Allen H. Eaton

Dean Of American Crafts

by

DAVID B. VAN DOMMELEN

David B. Van Dommelen (signature)

The Local History Company
publishers of history and heritage

Pittsburgh, Pennsylvania, USA

Allen H. Eaton:
Dean of American Crafts
Copyright © 2004 by David B. Van Dommelen

Published by
The Local History Company
112 North Woodland Road
Pittsburgh, PA 15232
www.TheLocalHistoryCompany.com
info@TheLocalHistoryCompany.com

The name "The Local History Company", "Publishers of History and Heritage", and its logo are trademarks of The Local History Company.

Front cover photograph of Allen H. Eaton ca. 1900 courtesy of Elizabeth and Martha Eaton.

Back cover photo of Allen H. Eaton in 1955 taken by Edward DuPuy. Courtesy of the Archives of Southern Highland Craft Guild and reproduced with the permission of Mr. DuPuy's estate.

Library of Congress Cataloging-in-Publication Data

Van Dommelen, David B.
    Allen H. Eaton : Dean of American Crafts / by David B. Van Dommelen.—1st American pbk. ed..
      p.   cm.
    ISBN 0-9711835-9-7 (pbk.: alk paper)
    1. Eaton, Allen H. (Allen Hendershott), b. 18 78 2. Handicraft—United States—History. 3. Oregon—Biography. I. Title.

TT140.E28V36 2003
745'.0973—dc21
                      2003013880

Printed in USA

d e d i c a t i o n

In Memory of Marian G. Heard
1908-2003
Director Emerita of
Arrowmont School of Arts and Crafts,
and friend to all craftsmen.

c o n t e n t s

acknowledgments

I want to thank Marian Heard posthumously for all her help in keeping me on track with my research and the writing of this book. She was an inspiration to me and to so many other craftspeople, both practicing artisans and writers in the field of crafts. Few people can be compared to her in her devotion to the development of crafts in the United States. Like Allen Eaton, she blazed many trails for artists and craftspeople who followed in her footsteps. I also wish to thank the following people and organizations; they all helped me in some way on the trip to the publication of this book.

Arrowmont School of Arts and Crafts

American Crafts Magazine

Berea College

Sandra Blain

Chicago Field Museum

Elizabeth and Martha Eaton

Chris Kiratzis

O.J. Mattil

Tina McMorran

John Niles

Louise Pitman

Oregon State University Library

Hal Riegger

The Franklin D. Roosevelt Library

The Russell Sage Foundation

Southern Highlands Craft Guild

Bernice Stevens

Kevin Thompson

Peggy Thompson

Charolette Waltz

Ann Wirth

I also want to thank Elizabeth and Martha Eaton posthumously for sharing with me their father's legacy of pictures, files, tapes and stories. Without them I could not have written this biography of their father. Special thanks go to Arthur Dervaes and Joanne Rutkowski for leading me to a publisher with vision and creative ideas. To my wife Michal Van Dommelen goes so much appreciation and love for her constant help through so many years in all my endeavors in publishing and making art.

David B. Van Dommelen

Introduction

I met Marian Heard in 1963, when she was the Director of Arrowmont School of Arts and Crafts, a position she held from 1945 to 1977. She was then also teaching in the Department of Crafts, Interior Design and Housing within the College of Home Economics at the University of Tennessee. As our relationship grew, she arranged for me to teach at Arrowmont. It was there, over cocktails before dinner with several staff members, that I learned about Allen Eaton. Marian Heard had long been involved with his work, and found him to be a person who should be recognized for his contributions to the field of the arts and crafts and for his search for beauty.

Because of Marian Heard's suggestion, I became intrigued with the work of Eaton by reading his book *Handicrafts of the Southern Highlands*. I discovered that he had also been deeply concerned with handicrafts and arts in many areas outside the Southern Highlands. As I talked to Marian over the years, I became convinced that he was indeed a man who warranted investigating in more depth, because his life's work had influenced this country's renaissance in the world of crafts, as well as its increased awareness of social, ethnic and cultural concerns.

I was not sure exactly how I wanted to study and investigate this man, but as I read his many articles and books, I felt I wanted to follow his voyage from the beginning and go chapter by chapter through his work. I started with his family; his daughters, who were still alive at that time, opened many doors for my research into what he had accomplished. They provided me with taped interviews along with many of the photographs included in this book.

As I exchanged letters and tapes with his daughters, and as I read his work, I realized that Eaton had played an important role in the resurgence of American crafts. When Eaton began to involve himself in the field of the arts, the world of crafts had degenerated into production of objects by the numbers. He was interested in the handicrafts of the individual and the beauty that these objects could bring to family life. He helped develop some of the major craft institutions, opened our eyes to the rich crafts of the United States, and brought aid and service to many countries around the world. He helped establish the Southern Highlands Craft Guild, guided the Pennsylvania Guild of Craftsmen in its infancy, and worked with the League of New Hampshire Craftsmen as it was founded. His work with Japanese-Americans and sightless people was testimony to his interest in beauty for all people.

Eaton was a simple, plain person, a man who had a mission, both for himself and for the future. He was not pretentious nor self-important, but ready to see, help and give support to other people. The "folks" of the Southern Highlands revered and worshiped him as he traveled among them, studying their ways.

There is no question that his title of "Dean of American Crafts" is well deserved.

The Early Years

In these unsuperstitious days no other ideal seems worthy of us, or indeed possible to us, save beauty— or call it, if you will, the dignity of human life . . .the teaching of what beauty is, to all . . .so that we wish and work and dream that not only ourselves, but everybody may be healthy and happy; and, above all, the fostering of the habit of doing things and making things well, for the joy of the work and the pleasure of achievement.

John Galsworthy

The Industrial Revolution and the era of Great Immigration exerted a profound influence on the development of the United States during the late 19th century and the early 20th century. The events of history which were to shape the character and the structure of this country during its adolescent years not only impressed themselves on the general developmental stages of cultural growth, social maturation, and economic exploitation, but also affected the lives of men and women who would contribute to the final coloration of this country. Among the impressive list of great Americans to enrich our social and cultural heritage was Allen Hendershott Eaton.

Allen Eaton through his publications and life's work clearly indicated that he was well aware of the nature of the country and of the time in which he lived. The Great Immigration, during the years of 1880 to 1900, was to set the stage for much of his work in attempting to elevate the arts, and at the same time in bringing about a better understanding of immigrant and ethnic gifts to this nation.

The year of Eaton's birth, 1878, was during the beginning of the onset of immigration to this country of peoples from every corner of the earth. Immigration was certainly not a new phenomenon, but its sheer volume during this era presented unique problems to the established population.

The problem was evident in the Far West, with the coming of Chinese and Japanese immigrants as labor forces during the settling of the Pacific coastal areas at the time of the Gold Rush, and for the building of the Transcontinental Railroad. In 1952, Eaton dedicated his book *Beauty Behind Barbed Wire* to the memory of his grandfather, The Honorable Jim Hendershott, who had " . . .in the 1880s on a date never recorded, but vividly remembered, 'uninvited' and in my small presence, met a posse of excited men in a grist mill in Grande Ronde Valley and persuaded them not to burn the houses and harm the Chinamen of our village who, at the time 'threatened' the existence of the United States with the 'Yellow Peril'."

Immigrants by the millions began to pour into America, and by 1888 an editorial in a New York newspaper stated that the flood gates and sewers were spewing the scum of immigration on our shores. This particular venom was pointed toward the Italian newcomers who numbered 12,000 in 1880 and 4,400,000 from 1880 on. They worked in construction jobs building the cities of an erupting nation, and they gave birth to the vineyards of California, New York and other locations. Along with the Italians came the Dutch, who not only helped settle this country in the early 1600s but in the late 1800s settled in Grand Rapids, Holland and Zeeland, Michigan, establishing lovely flower farms, and bringing furniture handicrafts which one day were to become synonymous with Grand Rapids.

While the Calvinist Dutch brought an "acceptable" Protestant religion, the Russian Jews brought another religion which was not as easily understood by the "native" Americans. Over one million Jews escaped the 1881-1903 pogroms in the Ukraine, Poland, and Lithuania, the so-called "Pale of Settlement." In total, Czarist Russia sent to our shores over 4,000,000 immigrants, most of whom were Jews. Also in 1890, 10,000 dissenters from the official Russian Orthodox Church settled in the Dakotas, and their evidence can be seen there today in the onion-like domes of the Mitchell, South Dakota Corn Palace.

Uprising against three of the most powerful monarchs in Poland brought thousands of Polish in 1830, 1849, and 1863. These Poles, along with those arriving in the late 1880s, found places in many parts of the United States in industrial jobs at wages that today would be considered criminally low.

The influx of Irish immigrants, who remained mostly on the eastern coast of the United States in major metropolitan areas, affected the direction of this country for the rest of its history. They became important in the labor forces acting in the capacities of straw bosses and foremen, but even more important, they found a niche for themselves in the political system of this country, at local levels, state levels and, finally, national levels.

Besides Irish, Poles, and Italians, European immigrants came from Sweden, Norway, Greece, Yugoslavia, and Germany. These groups brought with them a commitment to their past cultures, and many found geographic locations similar to their homelands. Like pockets in a woman's purse, they accumulated their idiosyncrasies and burst out upon the established American culture then almost 300 years old.

These burstings were to agitate and lacerate the existing communities and cultures, but in the end they were to influence the direction of Allen Eaton's work. He could not forget that they were there, and was drawn to them like iron to a magnet. His work with ethnic groups began with his *Arts and Crafts of the Homelands Exhibition* in 1919, and lasted through his work with the Japanese-Americans in relocation centers during the Second World War and until his death in 1962.

As these immigrants arrived, the American Industrial Revolution was in gear and accelerating at an incredible rate. The Industrial Revolution did not start in America, but it was the American Industrial Revolution which took it by the tail and threw it into the twentieth century. Joseph Paxton, an English architect and horticulturist, had already built the Crystal Palace in England in 1850. It had brought industry into the foreground as a viable force for science, finance, labor, and manufacturing. The machine was here to stay along with new techniques of building, and the inevitable result was mass production.

In the United States as the population surged westward railroads needed to be built, steel and iron had to be manufactured, and cities had to grow. America, indeed, engaged itself in becoming the most industrial of all nations.

As the machine and industrial age came into being toward the end of the 18th century, the gap of misunderstanding grew larger and larger, until consumers were compelled to buy objects produced by manufacturers who had no thought for the usefulness or beauty of the items. There were few articles on the market reflecting good design components. As an example, the textile mills in New England displaced home weaving.

The growing popularity of the machine and its increasing potential in production were paralleled by a sudden compulsion to invent. In the middle of the 19th century in England, persons in all areas of society were affected by this urge to create, while a similar surge swept across the United States. In all parts of Europe and the United States, men joined the restless pursuit of designing mechanical contrivances to exploit almost every human pursuit that can be imagined. Patent files full of records of this invention vogue attest to the variety and to the array of devices which played an important role in the evolution of our complex contemporary civilization. The arts suffered irreparable damage during this time, as creative vitality was diverted into this new mechanical experimentation; an indigenous art and craft failed to materialize during a time when native abilities were so ripe for development.

By the end of the nineteenth century the market was flooded with monstrously designed furnishings and crafts, and people purchased them because these products were the only ones available.

As the tempo of mass production and industrialization accelerated, it was evident that the relationship of the craftsman and the consumer would fall into disrepute. Products that once were based on human factors as well as material value, on close personal relationship between the craftsman and the consumer, were now impersonally manufactured in volume. Punching, pressing, stamping and casting were only a few of the new methods used to pour forth products from the factories into the hands of the public. The public had little or no understanding of evaluation. Its integrity was static, based on outmoded standards. The only positive result was the availability of mass-produced goods to many people with limited prior access.

With this degeneration and disintegration of design, industry, manufacturing, and consumer tastes, it was imperative that some new ideology be introduced to clear away the chaos and bring honest craftsmanship back into the limelight. Allen Eaton's entrance into the field of immigrant handicrafts was the beginning of the solution. Slowly, this farsighted man began his work, in order that we as a nation could have a better understanding of our pure creative potentials and our own heritage.

Before Eaton's entry into the field of handicraft promotion, there was some indication that not all crafts had disappeared. Small pockets of handicrafts could still be found throughout the country in rural areas and amongst some tribes of American Indians, although to a great extent these handicrafts were quickly vanishing. As native peoples were introduced to the white man's world of tools and objects, they were fast finding them more useful, though less beautiful, than their native handicrafts. However the more isolated tribes maintained at least minor production of traditional handicrafts.

The most significant art movement during Eaton's developing years was the period of Art Nouveau which had reached this country from Europe and flourished in many major cities. In this country it was labeled "The Arts and Crafts Movement," and extended roughly from 1870-1920. The strongest leaders in America were Louis Comfort Tiffany and Louis Sullivan. Neither were craftsmen in the traditional sense, but their philosophies wrapped around the craft concepts developing in this country.

Sullivan and his student Frank Lloyd Wright both utilized craftsmen in their architectural endeavors, but their use of carpenters, glass makers, and other craftsmen essentially did not do much to keep handicrafts as such alive.

Tiffany's work in home furnishing was more effective as a force for keeping handicrafts in the sight of the people. Tiffany was basically a decorator who called on the materials and techniques of the craftsmen to employ within the spaces he was designing. It was through his interest in textiles, wallpapers, lamp design, and other so-called minor arts, that his name became closely associated with handicrafts. Tiffany's fame was mainly spread through his development of *favrile* glass which he first used for windows, and later as lamp and household objects.

Tiffany and Eaton probably knew each other, although there is no specific documentation which substantiates this fact. Both lived in New York during the twenties, and both were good friends of Robert W. De Forest, who was president of the American Federation of Art and The Metropolitan Museum of Art in New York. De Forest not only recognized Eaton's important contributions to the field of exhibitions, but he and his family had also been deeply involved in the various decorative art groups associated with cultural developments in the New York and the American art world.

The applied arts, or those handicrafts and arts which were utilized by the decorators of the late 1800s and the early 1900s, were often made not by the decorator nor the designer himself, but instead were crafted in studios for the carriage trade. This was certainly true of most of Tiffany's work. There were many small prestigious and active groups devoting their time to developing design and handicrafts for decorators. The New York Society of Decorative Art was such a group, and an individual who was very active in this group was Gustav Stickley, the furniture designer who also published the short-lived *Craftsman* magazine.

Just prior to the emergence of Art Nouveau, there was an art movement for which William Morris can be held directly responsible. Morris was an English poet and artist who felt the need for revival and stimulation of the arts and crafts. He found that the age of industry had completely taken over the world of handicrafts and the result was a market flooded with cheap, gaudy, brash, and irresponsibly designed objects. Morris's idea was to arouse in the craftsman a creative and expressive force which would elicit a new art for the people.

In Joseph Gaston's *The Centennial History of Oregon*, published in 1912, Allen Eaton's work on the Pacific Coast is compared to Morris's Arts and Crafts Movement. Eaton is described as a person highly informed in the handiwork of England, France, and Germany, and one who applied and used them to promote happiness and beauty in the lives of the common people. Interestingly, Eaton had never traveled outside of Oregon when this was written.

Art Nouveau was not destined to remain a strong and vigorous movement. It only served as a stepping-stone to brighter and more permanent design philosophies in the handicrafts. It did, however, present a traditional world with a clue to the future in craft design. It helped bring about an awareness of the necessity of evaluating our position with the machine and industry.

Eaton was born May 10, 1878 in Union, Oregon, of pioneer parents. His father, John Burnham Eaton, Jr., was born in Vermont in 1849, and had come from New England searching for a new way of life. His mother, Minerva Patterson Hendershott, was the daughter of a man who had driven an oxen team to Oregon from Iowa in 1852 while his wife and children traveled via the Isthmus of Panama to join him. James Hendershott was later to serve in the Oregon House of Representatives, followed by two years as a state senator in 1868-1870. Service to the people was a trait which was to play a continual role in the lives of the Eatons and the Hendershotts.

Allen Eaton's grandfather married Rose Allen, a member of the family of Colonel Ethan Allen of Revolutionary War fame.

Union, Oregon was located in the County of Union and was founded in 1862. Grande Ronde Valley, in which the town is found, was the heart of agriculture and livestock farms of Eastern Oregon, and Merino sheep were raised on the hillside pastures of the Blue Mountains surrounding the valley. The population in the late 1880s ranged in the area of 1,500. Bernice Stevens of Gatlinsburg, Tennessee says, "Allen Eaton often spoke of how proud he was to have been born in a log cabin of pioneer parents."

Allen Eaton home on Fairmount Boulevard in Eugene, Oregon. Courtesy Lane County Pioneer Museum.

Union was far from a town of just log cabins. An important member of the Eaton family in Union was Abel E. Eaton, Allen Eaton's uncle. Abel Eaton was one of the wealthiest members of the community, and from the profits of his woolen mill in Union, and from his other enterprises, he was able to give a rather large endowment in 1908 to Willamette University in Salem, Oregon, which resulted in the building of Eaton Hall on that campus. One of Abel's interesting characteristics was his lack of faith in banks; he paid all his Union employees in gold and silver coin from a vault which he had built under the front parlor. The vault was discovered by Mr. & Mrs. David Rainey who were in the process of restoring the house to its original condition. Because of a family rift, Allen Eaton and his brothers never visited the Abel Eaton house until after the Raineys became the owners. This bit of family history, however, illustrates the milieu from which Allen Eaton came.

Allen H. Eaton, ca. 1900. Courtesy Elizabeth and Martha Eaton.

Allen Eaton's mother and grandmother were active as prohibitionists and suffragists, giving many speeches in the area and promoting women's causes. He especially enjoyed his grandmother's lovely flower garden which was filled with fruit trees and had peacocks wandering around the property.

When Eaton reached the age to enter his studies at the university, and graduated from the La Grande High School, he chose the University of Oregon over the Oregon Agricultural College (now Oregon State University) because the cost was $4.00 less. The four dollars was the cost of the uniform which was a requirement at the Agricultural College. His major contribution to the University of Oregon during his undergraduate years was his introduction of the *Webfoot*, the University's first annual yearbook, which he produced with his friend, E. N. Blythe. Eaton received his A.B. degree from the university in 1902 in the field of sociology and political science. Both areas of his studies would greatly affect his life in the years after his graduation. He put political science to practical use in a matter of just four years, but the application of his sociology took until 1920, when he became involved with the Russell Sage Foundation in New York City.

In 1903, the year after he graduated from the University of Oregon, he married Cecile Dorris, who was seven years his senior, and the daughter of Eugene, Oregon, resident Benjamin F. Dorris. In later years, Allen presented Benjamin Dorris' accumulated papers concerning the founding of the school and the appropriation of money for Deadly Hall, one of the first buildings to be erected on the campus in Eugene. An Oregon State park is also named after Ben and Kay Dorris. Two years after Eaton's marriage, Elizabeth was born to them, and after two more years Martha arrived. Both daughters in later years would play an active role in the arts.

In the fall of the year Eaton graduated from the University, he entered into one of the most unique businesses of the Northwest, according to Joseph Gaston's *The Centennial History of Oregon*. Eaton's Book and Art Store " . . .was established by him in order that he might have a wider opportunity for the expression of his ideals. His principal aim in life is to promote happiness and he believes this can best be accomplished perhaps by working along those lines of which the great English poet, William Morris, was the leading exponent. A person who is familiar with the genuine arts and crafts movement has said that Mr. Eaton already had done more to advance this movement than any other individual on the Pacific Coast."

Eaton was not the lone owner of the Art Store, but had a partner in this business adventure. Oscar Garrell went to China several times and brought back various art objects to be sold through the store. Garrell had been a classmate of Eaton's and had also served as an assistant on the staff of the *Webfoot*. When Eaton and Garrell opened this establishment, Eaton was a highly regarded citizen of Oregon, and the *Eugene Morning Register* in its Anniversary Edition of 1904 described the store:

> *Eaton's Book and Art Store, 545 Willamette Street, New McClung Bldg. This store, besides carrying the usual articles to be found at any book and stationery shop, 'was established' as Mr. Eaton puts it, 'for the purpose of making a living and bringing into town some things necessary and desirable in the book and art line, that people may get without going away from home . . .We believe it is our business to help makes homes beautiful, and believing this, we do not mean to carry many pictures and decorations that will tend to estrange husband and wife or drive a child away from its mother'.*

Eaton was deeply committed to the town of Eugene, the state of Oregon, and to the growth and development of the University of Oregon. These commitments intertwined in very complex ways, and from the time of his graduation from college until he left Oregon, contributions to the community and state were mixed with his interest in art and his concern for enriching the lives of the people around him, all of whom were surrounded by politics and political campaigns.

His book and art store grew, and by 1912 the Eugene directory listed two businesses for Eaton. By this time he had entered the bookbinding business and was also deeply involved in the political arena.

It was during these years that he acquired land on a ridge south of Eugene. At that time it was completely undeveloped, but afforded a magnificent view of the countryside. Documents indicate that he owned at various times between 12 and 20 acres.

He designed and built two houses on the north slope of the ridge. He and his family lived in one of these small but handsome houses, while the other house was occupied by Olive Newcomb, a prodigious potter. Eaton's house was situated at a higher point on the ridge, and a common road connected the two pieces of property with Fairmount Boulevard at the bottom of the hill. Today the former Eaton property is surrounded by the beautiful Hendrick Park which is maintained in a natural state full of flowering rhododendron and other plants and trees indigenous to Oregon.

In 1912, Eaton sponsored his first art exhibition by bringing borrowed paintings to Eugene. He felt he could begin to elevate the cultural level of a city far removed from the arts. This was the beginning of a long history in his life of providing art and craft exhibitions for the enrichment of people's lives all over the world. Earlier he had gone to the *Alaska-Yukon Exposition* of 1909 and brought one of Japan's finest painters to demonstrate in the store in Eugene.

One of Eaton's first really great achievements in the field of exhibitions was work with the exhibitions and display for the Oregon Building at the *Panama-Pacific International Exposition* in San Francisco in 1915. This was the same year that he was appointed to the faculty of the University of Oregon's School of Architecture, a result of his involvement with the arts and despite a lack of formal schooling in them.

Above: Oregon Pavilion at the 1915 Panama-Pacific Exposition, San Francisco, California. Oregon Historical Society, #OrHi 52518.

Below: Interior view of Oregon Pavilion at the Panama-Pacific Exposition design by Allen Eaton. Courtesy Elizabeth and Martha Eaton.

In *The Story of the Exposition* by Frank M. Todd, some of Eaton's exhibitions were described.

> *There was an art room in which everything, from curtains, furniture, and rugs to the paintings on the wall, was the work of Oregon artists and artisans, and some of it was most creditable. The woodwork was of Oregon cedar, and wall coverings were of an Oregon woolen resembling monk's cloth, the rugs were of native wool and woven in Oregon mills, and stained glass windows of Oregon glass and the designs by Oregon designers, and the pottery of Oregon clay. There was a handsome Oregon myrtle dining table, and there were chairs of the same beautiful material. On the walls were paintings, pastels, and watercolors by Oregon artists.*

Interestingly enough, one would expect the Panama-Pacific Exposition to set a new trend in the field of handicrafts and household arts, but outside of Eaton's work with the Oregon pavilion, there was little which impressed the people of this country who were concerned with the state of the handicrafts. In most of the reports of the exposition, little is mentioned about handicrafts except for a few minor displays in some of the foreign exhibition halls. Most of the state exposition buildings concerned themselves with agriculture, industrial development, and general historical displays. The total exposition grounds were more heavily weighted toward the fine arts. Most buildings in the fair exhibited famous paintings and sculptures brought to San Francisco from various national museums and galleries. It is probably for this reason that Eaton's displays in the Oregon building received national fame in many publications.

In 1917, *The International Studio* magazine published an article "Art in Toys", which was specifically about Allen Eaton's family and their contributions to the Oregon exhibitions in terms of miniature objects they had built. Besides a beautifully crafted miniature Noah's Ark, with all the animals intact, there was also a delightful farm with its animals and a lovely doll house. In later years, the Eaton family would continue their interest in handicrafts through the use of miniatures in the form of music boxes, although this project was mostly a business interest of Eaton's daughter, Martha.

Eaton's entry into the world of teaching art was at a very significant time. Around the turn of the twentieth century and in the latter part of the nineteenth century, art education and craft education began to emerge as a part of curricula in public schools and in institutions of higher education. Until this period, art was seldom a strong part of the educational system, and usually was taught as drawing courses and pure fine art classes.

The movement which brought craft education into the schools began with the work of Arthur Dow and the writings of Charles A. Bennett. Many other authorities were bringing forth new philosophies and materials which were giving attention to the manual training courses, handicrafts, domestic arts, and industrial arts. Eaton began his teaching when the whole concept of education was changing. Not only were art courses beginning to recognize that the applied arts had an important role in aesthetic training, but home economics was being formed by scientist Ellen H. Richards, who strongly supported beauty as an integral portion of a family's life as part of her interest in euthenics.

Along with Dow and Bennett, other educators joined the push to bring art education and craft education into a more vital part of the schools. The term "manual training" came into being because of this new surge in understanding the manual arts as related to education. It was probably Walter J. Kenyan who can be credited with the first use of the term "handicrafts." In 1899, Kenyon's book *First Years in Handicraft* was published, and its use became common language thereafter.

Eaton used the term "handicraft" continually in his work, rather than "crafts." In his "Preface" to *Handicrafts of the Southern Highlands*, Eaton defines the word:

> . . . 'handicraft,' as used in this report, is a broad
> term including all those things which people make
> with their hands either for their own use or for that
> of others. The article may be fashioned entirely by
> hand, including the preparation of all materials even
> to the shaping of the tools employed, or it may be
> made in part by machinery as in the preparation of
> woods for fine cabinet work, or as in the machine
> spinning of thread and yarn to be woven on the
> hand loom; but if the final product, the character of
> the thing itself, is shaped by hand it is an object of
> handicraft . . .

It was also at the *St. Louis Exposition* in 1904 that more impetus was given art and craft education through exhibitions and presentations of new ideas in handicraft philosophies, although this did not seem to influence the 1915 *Panama-Pacific International Exposition* in any way.

The interest in handicraft education could be felt very strongly in the East, and there were some evidences of it affecting the West Coast, but by 1900 the need for a magazine which would promote art instruction was apparent. The outcome was the *Applied Arts Book* which was retitled in 1902 to *School Arts*. In later years, this magazine would publish many of Eaton's articles.

Eaton entered the Oregon State Legislature in 1907, his first attempt at public office. His seat in the Legislature represented Lane County where the city of Eugene and the University of Oregon were situated. His concerns were many, ranging from his strong campaign to bring a municipal and controlled water system to Eugene to better appropriations for the University. In 1949, Senator Wayne Morse described him as the "personification of statesmanship."

During his tenure in the State Legislature, Eaton served on many important House standing committees, as well as special legislative committees. Included were Ways and Means (1907-1909); Education (1909); Rules and Joint Rules (1909, 1913, 1915) plus many others, making him a strong adversary in the House of Representatives. He introduced innumerable bills, both alone and jointly with other representatives. He introduced a bill to provide for the incorporation and organization of public utility districts, and sponsored a bill to establish a state employment bureau.

One of the most controversial of his activities was his campaign to increase appropriations for the University of Oregon. In December, 1949, an *Old Oregon* columnist recapped the story of Eaton's fight: " . . .it was his effort that brought an assured annual provision of $125,000 to the University within a few years after he received his A.B. in Sociology and Political Science."

The University was then receiving $47,000 annually, the lowest amount provided by any state in the Union. Eaton, who had served two terms as president of the Alumni Association, resolved to do something in return for his education.

He introduced a bill for a provision of $125,000 to be spent at the regents' discretion, and he mustered enough support to put it before the governor for his signature.

Governor George Chamberlain, who, in Eaton's view was the most popular governor Oregon had ever seen, vetoed the measure. It was then passed by both houses of the legislature over the veto, and soon referred to the voters through a referendum petition.

Eaton's immersion into state government and politics was total, and he was intensely keen about Oregon's Initiative and Referendum system of governing. In 1912, at the age of 34, he wrote his first book, *The Oregon System: The Story of Direct Legislation in Oregon*, published by A. C. McClurg & Co. in Chicago. Eaton was hopeful that his book would be an unprejudiced examination of the work which the people of Oregon had accomplished since the adoption of the system in 1902.

In the book, Eaton discusses the sixty-four measures which had passed and been placed on the ballot during the years 1904 to 1912. He pointed out the pros and cons of the system, and in one chapter discusses various aspects of the popular election of United States senators.

While he stated in his Preface to the book, "The task of presenting the facts as they are is a worthy undertaking, particularly since I do not know of any one else who has tried to give the history from this unprejudiced standpoint", he failed completely whenever he discussed the University of Oregon and relevant legislation. His love for his Alma Mater consistently showed through, and lasted until his death, even though five years after the publication of the book, he was forced to leave the university.

The Oregon System, however, was a book which was able to place the political system of Oregon in a good perspective, and at an early date in its growth.

By the summer of 1917, Eaton was well-known to the people of Oregon. He made his reputation not only in the university community, but in the town of Eugene as well. His work in State government was well-known, and he had established himself as a writer. He was considered an important asset to the state, and had fought for the rights of the little man. At the same time, he had made many enemies in his various contests for better conditions for the citizens of Oregon. Here was a university professor, a state legislator, a young businessman, but even more important, a man who deeply believed that beauty and art were essential elements for all people to live happy and satisfying lives. What more could a young man dream of as a goal for his aspirations?

In the *Oregon Voter* of May 13, 1917, the following description of Eaton was published in view of the upcoming elections.

ALLEN EATON, who has served longer continuously in the House than any other member, will probably run pretty strong, as he is well-known and a great campaigner. Eaton has been the minority candidate for Speaker since the memory of man runneth not to the contrary. He wore out his influence by his obstructive tactics, although his ability as a debater was such that in the latest session Speaker Spelling feared him more than any other man on the floor. Eaton is a keen parliamentarian, a speaker of unusual eloquence, and a veritable encyclopedia of legislative information. Yet his tongue is so sharp that he antagonized most members, and repeatedly stirred up severe opposition to the university, of which he was the special advocate.

With the successes that he had, and the happy life that he was living, it was impossible to consider that this phase of his life would end in one of the biggest controversies to hit the State of Oregon since its acceptance into the United States of America in 1859.

This controversy would appear and reappear in almost every review of his books published decades later. It would be a controversy that would always lie under the surface of any event related to Eaton and to his association with Oregon and Eugene, Oregon, specifically. The citizenry of the State and of Eugene would select sides like a 4th of July picnic tug of war. To this day, the events are not always clear, and written reports of either side are considered biased.

Eaton's teaching position at the University of Oregon ended abruptly when he was forced by the University's Board of Regents to hand in his resignation because he had attended a meeting of the People's Council for Democracy and Peace in Chicago on September 2, 1917.

October 4, 1917

My Dear President Campbell:

I herewith hand to you my resignation as a member of the faculty of the University of Oregon, with the request that it be placed before the board of regents for their consideration as soon as they shall be able to meet in full board session. At that time I shall respectfully ask the privilege of personally appearing before the board to answer the charges that have been brought against me by the Eugene Chamber of Commerce.

I deeply regret that the board of regents should have forced upon them this unpleasant and unmerited responsibility. I tried to avoid it for the University by offering to lay before the Chamber Commerce all the facts in the case, that they might have an opportunity to modify or withdraw the demand that was made without a knowledge of the truth, but this offer was refused. Now that the University must take the responsibility of this investigation, I desire to do what I can to give the board freedom for their action, and to save the University from unjust agitation and pressure.

As I see it, there are only two big considerations in the whole matter. One is the welfare of the University, the other is justice to me. I put the University first because I want it to be considered first and because it is important to more people. But the clearing of my name of false charges is both important to the University and vital to me. Therefore, I shall welcome the opportunity that I know will be granted to me to place the whole truth before the regents, believing that the truth and freedom will bring justice.

Nothing in this communication must be construed as an admission of any alleged facts that I have already denied; it is an admission only of my confidence in the board of regents whose anxiety to serve the University cannot be greater than mine. I will appreciate an early meeting.

Respectfully yours
Allen Eaton

According to some reports, Eaton stopped only to observe the People's Council for Democracy and Peace meeting on his return to Oregon after a summer job he had in the east as Director of the Wyoming, New York, Summer School of Arts & Life. Other reports place him as a delegate representing Wyoming, New York. America had declared war on Germany on April 6th, and by the summer, troops were already in Europe. Both the Emergency Peace Federation and later the People's Council were deeply opposed to the war and were extremely verbal about their ideological and political concerns. According to some reports, Eaton had also attended one of the People's Council meetings at Madison Square Garden in New York City.

The People's Council was a pacifist organization with leftist and socialist leanings, and by July of 1917 it had been branded a pro-German socialist organization by the New York area conservative press. By June 13, 1917, The Emergency Peace Federation had been absorbed into the People's Council at a meeting in Swarthmore, Pennsylvania; by the time of a July meeting in Chicago, where several thousands of people gathered along with the Chicago Peace Convention of the Socialist Party, its reputation was well-known. Samuel Gompers of the A.F. of L. and the initiator of the A.F. of L. Peace Alliance was its greatest protagonist.

Eaton's attendance at the September meeting came to the knowledge of Oregonians when he contributed a short article concerning the meeting to the September 4 *Oregon Journal*, a Portland, Oregon, newspaper.

Delegates to the People's Council for Democracy and Peace are today leaving for their several states confident that in time the people of the country will know the truth about the organization and the methods used to prevent the members from meeting.

The two meetings which have been held, together with the work of the executive committee agreed to meet secretly.

Much greater than the issues involved in the People's Council has loomed the refusal of the governor of Illinois to permit the citizens to assemble and speak. None of the officers or members of the organization were ever permitted to place the case before the executive, who finally took the position that while the convention might be peaceable enough, no doubt mobs would incite riots. At the meeting held while the governor was rushing hundreds of soldiers to Chicago and securing guns and ammunition, not a single disturber was present and the two policemen on guard at the hall seemed unnecessary. Resolutions were passed by the council to accept the president's reply to the Pope as the first clear definite statement of the war attitude of this country and asked that the allied nations do likewise and that we do not demand a larger measure of democracy for Germany than we allow to ourselves.

By September 13, the Eugene, Oregon Commercial Club (Chamber of Commerce), supported by the Spanish-American War Veterans and a committee of mothers whose sons were already in Europe, presented a series of charges of disloyalty against Eaton. This resolution was formally filed on October 29, 1917, to the Board of Regents of the University of Oregon.

Whereas, Allen H. Eaton, a member of the faculty of the University of Oregon, was a delegate to the meeting of the People's Council for Democracy and Terms of Peace, an organization reputed to be disloyal to the national cause and best serving the designs of the German government in creating the impression in Russia that the people of the United States are not united in the war, and

Whereas, Allen H. Eaton subscribed to the principles of the People's Council, publicly defending the action taken at its Chicago meeting, held in defiance of the governor of the state of Illinois and against the best interest of the United States, and

Whereas, it has been announced the members of the faculty of the University of Oregon had circulated a petition asking that Allen H. Eaton be retained as a member of the faculty of the University and stated that this petition denounces pro-German propaganda and condemns the People's Council but asserts the faith of the petitioners in the loyalty of Mr. Eaton as an American citizen, be it,

Resolved, that we as mothers of boys who are serving in the various branches of the army and navy condemn the conduct of Allen H. Eaton, and be it further

Resolved, that we cannot accept the denunciation of German propaganda and condemnation of the People's Council by other members of the faculty of the University of Oregon as having any connection with Mr. Eaton's case inasmuch as Mr. Eaton, himself, does not express his condemnation of the People's Council and its action which has been interpreted by patriotic Americans as German propaganda, and be it further

Resolved, that we believe the interests of the state, the nation and our sons who are now in service of their country will best be served by the acceptance of

Mr. Eaton's resignation as a member of the faculty of the University of Oregon, and be it further

Resolved, that the chairman of this meeting appoint a committee of three to present a copy of these resolutions to the board of regents of the University of Oregon at the meeting of that body tomorrow night.

The Eugene Chamber of Commerce resolution also went to the Governor of Oregon; this version went further in that it asked the Governor to remove Eaton from his seat in the House of Representatives because Eaton had signed his article "Allen Eaton, representative in the legislature of Oregon from Lane County."

Even though these allegations were never proven, the Board of Regents of the University of Oregon did not bend. Of the six motions and two amendments made, none were unanimous. Of the 13 members of the Board of Regents, only nine were present. Governor James W. Withycombe was not present. Eight members did vote for the acceptance of Eaton's resignation, which was dated October 4, 1917.

The faculty also presented the Board of Regents a petition, signed by a large contingent of the faculty, and supported but not signed by the University President, Price L. Campbell. Their petition attempted to persuade the regents to retain Eaton and pointed, to some extent, the finger of blame on the Eugene Chamber of Commerce.

During the period of time that Eaton returned and before the Regent's meeting, Eaton attempted to have a public meeting where he could defend himself, but he was barred the use of both a local Presbyterian church and the Lane County Courthouse by deputy sheriffs. Eaton claimed that he wanted an opportunity to speak to the Chamber of Commerce, but was refused, and that he was not informed of the meeting time, even though he was a member of the Commercial Club. This action, and the action of the Board of Regents, were moves that even today some people consider a permanent blot on the history of Eugene and the University.

Oswald G. Villard, editor and president of the *New York Evening Post*, wrote a defense of Eaton in the November 15, 1917 *Nation*, concerning the "infringement of the professorial right of independence of speech and conscience," and appealed to the American Association of University Professors that here was a case worthy of attention. However, the Association never directly took his case, but they did make a few generalizations about freedom of speech.

In the Report of the President in the November 1917 issue of the AAUP *Bulletin*, the president reports that letters had been received calling attention " . . .to the action which has in a few cases been taken against members of faculties on account of their public utterances with reference to the war . . . ." And in the February-March 1918 issue of the same publication, an article concerning "Academic Freedom in Wartime", encourages "fair trial" by allowing the accused to state his case before a judicial committee. But at no time did the Association act in a positive manner to help and defend those professors who were rightly speaking their ideas. Eaton's case had drawn considerable national attention in New York newspaper and other political and social science publications.

Eaton's only fault, apparently, was that he attended the meeting as an observer, reported it openly to the public, and then was condemned for his actions. Because Eaton was well-known in Oregon, and especially because of his many active years in the State Legislature, he was defended by *The Spectator* of Portland, Oregon:

> *No, the Regents could not accuse Mr. Eaton of intending disloyalty to his government, or to his university, or to his city, or to the humblest decent person or thing on earth . . . Allen Eaton could no more harbor a disloyal, dishonorable, or dishonest thought than the fixed stars could change their courses in the skies . . . Practically every member of*

*the splendid faculty of which Mr. Eaton has been
an honor and an ornament expressed unwavering
faith in his loyalty. There was the real test; and there
was the fine, unequivocal heart-filling answer to the
allegation of envy, jealousy and enmity.*

Probably one of the most famed reports of Eaton's case came
when Upton Sinclair published his book *Goose-Step, A Study
of American Education* in 1923. Martin Schmitt, former Librarian of Special Collections at The University of Oregon, states,
"This episode is very inaccurately reported in Upton Sinclair's
Goose-Step"; yet continuously throughout newspaper articles
from various parts of the country, it appears accurate, including Sinclair's method of tying it to political maneuvers by local
politicians.

Sinclair states, " . . .so the special interests of Oregon were
out to 'get' him at any price." This remark refers to different
events which Sinclair writes about in terms of varied legislation and movements that Eaton fought for in order to help the
citizens of Lane County. In many of these issues he was directly
opposed to the commercial and business interests, even though
he was a Republican.

The issue which Sinclair specifically writes about is the problem of the city water. It was this event which forced Eaton into
politics, according to Sinclair.

*There was an epidemic of typhoid in the town of
Eugene, and eighty of the students were ill, and more
than two hundred of the townspeople—twenty-two of
them died within a fortnight. Mr. Eaton ascertained
from the physicians of the town that the city water
was contaminated, and so he published an article
advising everyone to boil the water before drinking it.
The water supply was controlled by a private water
company, in which the banks were interested, along
with prominent members of the Eugene Commercial*

Club. Mr. Eaton's banker and others of these citizens undertook to 'persuade' him to keep quiet about the epidemic; 'so much talk is giving the town a black eye'. They made threats which forced the young professor either to 'knuckle down' or to fight in the open. He chose the latter course, and he forced municipal ownership of the water works; a modern filtration system was installed and in ten years there has not been a single case of typhoid traceable to the city water....

These and other issues according to Sinclair brought the Commercial Club after Eaton, and when he finally opened himself for criticism during the controversy of the People's Council, they attacked.

Just how extensively this event was precipitated by political enemies is not known. However, there is little doubt that Eaton's involvement in important policy-making legislature was deep, and there is every right to consider the fact that big industry and banking concerns would attempt to unseat him from the State Legislature and make him appear undesirable in his community by any method they found most convenient.

Eaton's expulsion from the University made a deep and lasting impression on the town of Eugene, Oregon, for seldom has anything been written about him after he left Eugene that did not attempt to mention this event, and also seemed to be apologizing for what the town's attitude had been. As late as December 22, 1975, when an article was written about Eaton by Marvin Tims, letters were received by the local paper making various comments about freedom and repression.

On November 13, 1949, a review of his book *Handicrafts of New England*, in the *Eugene Register Guard* stated

... Allen Eaton fought a battle here for freedom of speech and opinion. He was kicked out of the University of Oregon for being 'pacifist and

*pro-German' . . .Oregon was not the only community
in the United States to be stirred to frenzy when we
first went to war with Germany. At Harvard, our
most ancient citadel of free opinion, windows were
stoned. From coast to coast ran a wave of patriotic
hysteria. The Eaton episode was only one of many
sad manifestations of national immaturity. We think
we have grown up a little.*

During the Second World War, only seven years before this
article appeared, Oregon was one of the states that deported
their Japanese-American citizens to relocation centers where
some were held until 1946, three years before the date of the
article claiming a new level of maturity.

Again, in the *Register Guard* on the 28th of February, 1952,
when his book *Beauty Behind Barbed Wire* was reviewed,
the fact that " . . .Mr. Eaton himself experienced persecution
during World War I right here in Eugene" was inserted in the
article.

Probably the most significant article published was carried
in the *Oregon Voter* of November 2, 1917, when it projected
Eaton's destiny.

*Why demolish a man just because he is visionary
and impractical? Eaton always meant well. Now he
has to quit the little salary upon which he depended,
quit the institution he loved and become a professional
martyr . . . Those who persecuted him did neither
country nor state a service. For their persecution of
him they have laid the foundation for a future career,
with all the disaffected elements of society beholding
him as a leader . . . And this bullying of poor Allen
Eaton may make him an Oregon character who will
have to be reckoned with seriously in the future. For
dreamers are dangerous when they are not permitted
to dream in peace. Dreamers have overturned*

governments and established new social orders. They
are not bad fellows when left alone, but make martyrs
of them and from the burning stake they speak words
that topple dynasties.

Eaton did not leave Eugene or Lane County at once. He still
had unfinished business. He was still up for reelection in the
May 1918 election, and he stayed in order to fulfill his interests
and obligations. Still, the elements who wanted him out continued to push him. On May 11, 1918, six days before the election,
an article appeared in the *Oregon Voter* titled "Disgrace to
Oregon," a reversal of their November 1917 stand:

> *Lane County will not disgrace herself by nominating*
> *Allen H. Eaton for the Legislature. At least, we so*
> *believe. Mr. Eaton belongs to the LaFollette class*
> *for patriotism. The issue was made clearly when he*
> *replied to the charges upon which he was released*
> *from his position with the University. His reply*
> *revealed a lack of understanding of the fundamental*
> *principles of patriotism and a willingness to affiliate*
> *with conscientious objectors and others whose*
> *aim was to discredit our war. Lane County people*
> *unquestionably realize that his nomination would be*
> *as shameful a blot upon the reputation of the county*
> *as would have been the nomination of the LaFollette*
> *candidate by the state of Wisconsin. With three*
> *candidates to nominate from a field of five there is a*
> *possibility that he might squeeze in unless the Lane*
> *County people make such an issue of his candidacy*
> *that none will vote for him knowingly unless they*
> *desire to disgrace the county.*

On September 14, 1920, Eaton wrote to his friend Eric Allen,
Dean of the School of Journalism at the University of Oregon:

May 17, 1918	*Defeated in Republican primaries for State Representative by David Graham, L.E Bean, James Fullerton and others.*
May 18, 1918	*Left Eugene for New York*
May 27, 1918	*Arrive in Washington Square New York with family and $20. With promise of another loan if necessary. Knew five people in the city but didn't want to see them 'till (sic) I got a job.*

The Russell Sage Foundation

Inasmuch as ye have done it to the least of these my brethren, ye have done it unto me.

Motto of the Russell Sage Foundation

Russell Sage Building in New York City. Photo by the author.

Allen Eaton joined the staff of the Russell Sage Foundation in 1920, and after 26 years of service, he left at the age of 68. It was during these Foundation years that he began to establish himself as an expert in craft development.

On the death of Russell Sage, July 22, 1906, his wife Margaret Olivia Sage received the total amount of his earnings, $65,000,000, which had come from many varied sources, among them railroad bonds and real estate in Manhattan.

Sage's widow immediately began to consider ways in which she could dispose of the money to charitable organizations and concerns. As she approached this awesome task, she did it with as much care as she could. She surrounded herself with several advisors, but especially depended on her attorneys, Robert W. and Henry W. De Forest. She received thousands of request letters and ideas for hundreds of ways in which she could donate her money. Each was carefully considered before any steps were taken to invest it in such affairs.

On December 10, 1906, Robert De Forest suggested that she establish a Sage Foundation, and in the ensuing few months work went ahead on just such a project. By April 11, 1907, then New York Governor Charles E. Hughes signed into being the charter for the Russell Sage Foundation.

While De Forest had suggested the name Sage Foundation, the name finally chosen was the Russell Sage Foundation. Mrs. Sage was very vehement that the money used for the Foundation and other future memorials would be in Russell Sage's memory and not in honor of herself. In 1906, only eight other foundations existed in the United States, and of these, only two were equal in capital funds to the Russell Sage Foundation.

The initial endowment which Mrs. Sage put into the Foundation was $10,000,000, but at the time of her death on November 4, 1918, she bequeathed another $5,000,000. Other monies were given, much during her last few years, to the Sage Institute of Pathology, the Susana Hospital in Guam, a park and playground which she maintained in Sag Harbor, Long Island, a shelter for migratory birds in the State of Louisiana, planting of rhododendrons in Central Park, and many other causes.

De Forest's initial purpose for suggesting the Foundation was "Social Betterment," but Mrs. Sage defined her hopes and ideals in April 19, 1907 in a letter which accompanied the endowment.

> *The scope of the Foundation is not only national but is broad. It should, however, preferably not undertake to do that which is now being done or is likely to be effectively done by other individuals or by other agencies. Its aim should be to take up the larger and more difficult problems and to take them up so far as possible in such a manner as to secure co-operation and aid in their solution.*

The news of the establishment of the Foundation was received favorably by social workers, educators, and the press. These groups were especially pleased with the unlimiting factors of the endowment and its possible contributions to future scientific knowledge of the conditions of man. However, during the first trustee meeting, limitations were placed on the work of the Foundation and these limitations fell into three categories. It was decided that the Foundation would not "attempt to relieve individual or family need," "give no aid to universities and colleges," nor "give aid to churches for church purposes."

It was not long before work was well on the way to constructing the general policies of the Foundation, organizing the structure of departments, and developing the many programs which were to be a part of the future organization. By 1910, the Foundation listed the following departments as active participating units: Charity Organization, Child Hygiene, Child Helping, Editorial; the departments of Recreation, Education,

Southern Highlands, Remedial Loans, and Industrial Studies were in the process of being formed.

Interestingly enough, Eaton's contributions at the Foundation did not take place in the Southern Highlands Division, as one would expect because of his book on crafts in the Southern Highlands. Instead, they were in the Division of Arts and Social Work, which he formed. The Department of Southern Highlands came to an abrupt halt May 2, 1919, on the death of John C. Campbell, who had been its director since its inception in October 1912. This division through the guidance of Campbell had been deeply concerned with the economic and educational needs of the Highlands, and Mrs. Olive Dame Campbell was totally immersed in the mountain lore of the region. On the death of Campbell, his uncompleted manuscript *The Southern Highlander and His Homeland* was finished by Mrs. Campbell and published by the Foundation.

The fact that Campbell had already set a precedent on work in the Southern Highlands made Eaton's work easier after he arrived on the scene at the Foundation. It was through Mrs. Campbell's invitation that Eaton entered into his studies of the Southern Highlands.

Eaton did not begin his work with the Russell Sage Foundation immediately upon his arrival in New York in the spring of 1918, however. He was desperate for work and money with which he could support his family, so he took a position with a furniture factory for $100.00 a month.

After working in that capacity for a few months, he took a position as Senior Examiner for the Emergency Fleet Corporation of the States of New York, New Jersey, and Connecticut. In a May 18, 1944 report to the Trustees of the Russell Sage Foundation he discussed these activities.

> *The work with the Emergency Fleet Corporation, which was a part of the U.S. Shipping Board, was the prevention of strikes and lockouts and their earliest adjustment when they did occur in New York, New*

Jersey, and part of New England for then, as today, the great job was to keep production going on the home front. This work brought me into continuous touch with countless foreign citizens, many of whom could not speak our language, but who like their sons and brothers in the armed services had the spirit of Americanism in their heart and the will to make any sacrifice. Many of these workers in the war plants revealed, often through interpreters, some of the finest human qualities and a loyalty to America which I could never forget. And often I could see background and cultural traditions of great value among these immigrants.

His work, according to a letter he sent to Eric Allen in Eugene, Oregon, was very satisfactory to both employers and employees of the E.F.C. He remained at this position until May 1, 1919, when he

. . . accepted position Field Secretary for American Federation of Arts (first time created) Salary $4000. Proposed and organized for the University of the State of New York Series of Exhibitions of Arts and Crafts of the Homelands, as a part of the Americanization program. This was said by Christian Science Monitor and authorities on the subject to be the best type of Americanization work yet done in the country. Also organized the first complete exhibition of Prints in Color and Photographs for American Homes, for the Federation and opened the initial exhibition at Russell Sage Foundation in January 1920.

In the same letter to Eric Allen, he continued,

June 1, 1920, Accepted position Associate Director Department of Surveys and Exhibits, Russell Sage Foundation, Salary $5000, with time for outside

work. (The salary matter I knew would please you but it is at present confidential). Engaged now in writing the story of the exhibitions of the Arts and Crafts of the Homelands, to be published by the Foundation. Will send you a copy if you wish.

Well that's about all and more too. I expect within a few months to find the Foundation the most useful work I have been able to do and I will write you more of it as it develops.

During Eaton's first years with the Foundation, he kept in close touch with his friends in Oregon, and he wrote many letters to Ellis F. Lawrence, the Dean of Journalism at the University. He often spoke in these letters about Oregon and his house in Eugene, but most of all he reported to them about his new position. Eaton was a great correspondent throughout his life. His letters would ramble in delightful ways and in a rather homespun philosophic manner. His yearly Christmas letters to friends, which he duplicated usually by mimeograph, are full of interesting tales about his experiences during the year in which the letter was written.

When Eaton first arrived at the Foundation, his primary concern was

To bring into the field of social work a greater appreciation of the vital relation of art and beauty to life . . . He believed social work could be strengthened and enriched by a wider recognition of the power of the arts, in a broad sense, and that the arts could gain if there was a clearer conception of the social function. The problem was to find out how the arts could be practically applied to social work.

(Glenn, p. 369)

The Department of Survey and Exhibits was established in 1912 and continued its activities until 1943. Its primary purposes were to investigate, study, and develop social surveys and the social exhibit as tools for community improvement. Shelby Harrison, who was the director of this department wrote that the purpose,

> . . . *was something more than the centralizing of inquiries regarding surveys and exhibits. Behind that was a conviction that the survey, including the exhibit and other popular methods of educating the public, was proving a sound and effective measure for preventing and correcting conditions that are wrong, and for quickening community forces that are showing promise. It was recognized that important changes in our national life and community relationships . . . had brought new problems calling for study and that in dealing with the new needs the usefulness of the survey as an organized method of social discovery and analysis, and the exhibit as an agency for popular interpretation had been demonstrated.*

> (Glenn, p. 177)

Most of the exhibits worked on during the duration of the department dealt with social concerns around the United States. Surveys and exhibits were conducted in Springfield, Illinois; Peoria, Illinois; Newburgh, New York; Topeka, Kansas, and many other sites. Each covered various problems of the particular communities and involved the citizens of each area. While these activities were important in the operations of the Survey and Exhibits Department, they did not relate to the major part of Eaton's interest until later in the history of the Foundation, when arts and crafts were a part of the designated operations and programs.

Because of the way Eaton had performed in the area of exhibits, such as the 1915 *Exposition* in San Francisco and the *Arts and Crafts of the Homelands* exhibit in Buffalo, De Forest felt he was well-suited for the position which the Foundation was offering. Eaton accepted the job. He worked diligently within the department, but as we will see, his work slowly moved toward the establishment of another division within the Foundation which he would someday head himself. From the time of Eaton's arrival, and until the Department of Arts and Social Work came into being, there was a dual purpose in Eaton's work with Surveys and Exhibits.

One of Eaton's first tasks after he went to the Foundation was to begin writing a publication covering his work on the *Art and Crafts of the Homelands* exhibitions in which he had been so involved before his appointment and for several years after his appointment to the Foundation. The eventual publication of *Immigrant Gifts to American Life* was the result of this work.

But the most significant work to come out of the Department of Survey and Exhibits during Eaton's involvement and before his *Immigrant* book was a bibliography of social surveys of the New York City area. This monumental undertaking greatly infringed on Eaton's work in handicrafts, but utilized his sociological training which he had received in his undergraduate years at the University of Oregon. In John M. Glenn's *History of the Russell Sage Foundation 1907-1947*, he describes the study in a development report to the Foundation Board of Trustees.

> When in 1921 the Foundation initiated its general survey of the New York Region, Mr. Harrison naturally had important responsibilities for that project. No more surveys were undertaken by the department, but it continued to keep its information up to date, to confer on plans of surveys, and to suggest persons competent to direct them.

> Printed materials on surveys had increased so much since the Department published the revised edition of its bibliography in 1915, that in 1918 preparation of another revision was begun. After Mr. Eaton joined the staff, the search for items and the laborious detail of preparing and classifying entries were mainly his responsibility. Publication was delayed from year to

year, partly because of the wealth of material and of constant changes of classification. When at length it was issued it was a substantial book, listing 2,775 projects completed to January, 1928. An introduction by Mr. Harrison reviewed the survey movement from its beginning, analyzing the trends that had taken place since 1907, offering 'an attempt at a definition of the survey and its purpose' and discussing 'the significance of surveys as a means of informing citizens regarding community condition.'

(Glenn, p. 354)

While Eaton and Harrison were working on the compilation of this survey, they were asked by the Welfare Council of New York City to assemble a bibliography of studies made in New York from 1915 to 1925. This publication was finished and published in August 1926. A list of 527 reports was included in 84 pages, and was published by the Welfare Council of New York as *Welfare Problems in New York City: A Bibliography of Social Surveys*; however, it was not published until 1930 by the Foundation. In 1976, this publication was reissued by Arno Press in New York.

During the first ten years of Eaton's work with the Foundation, and while he struggled to publish his book *Immigrant Gifts to American Life*, handicrafts were not emphasized greatly in the United States. Little was seen of handicrafts by the general public, although underlying the American scene was a constant stream of handicrafts being produced in all parts of the country. Most of these were being produced by rural people, ethnic groups, and often by homemakers enriching their family lives. Eaton was very much aware of these handicrafts when he assembled the exhibition of Oregon objects for the Oregon Building at the *Panama-Pacific Exposition* in 1915, and the *Arts and Crafts of the Homelands Exhibition* in Buffalo in 1919.

Though at first glance it appeared that little effort was being extended toward the handicrafts while Eaton worked on his social surveys, there were two institutions which would significantly contribute to the development of handicrafts in future years.

Of real importance for the development of handicrafts was an institution in Germany which played a worldwide role not only in handicraft development, but in architecture, graphics, painting, design education, and other related fields of study. The whole question about a Bauhaus influence in the field of handicrafts is ethereal to say the least, for it is difficult to concretely show direct influence. However, by 1960, there were few people in the art world who would not support the fact that indeed the Bauhaus school's role in influencing the arts in this country was the most significant influence of the twentieth century. Oskar Schlemmer, in his diary in June 1923, wrote that the Bauhaus was an experiment bringing the arts and crafts and academic art together. It was a pioneer in the field of craft education. To Schlemmer, four years of Bauhaus was a major portion in the history of art. They were a part of social history, reflecting the fermenting human situation of a nation and a period.

In addition to architecture, design, and painting studios, students and faculty in pottery and weaving studios began to examine the crafts as tools to improve industry and the manufacturing of commercial objects. Henry van der Velde, known for his work in the Art Nouveau movement, looked toward crafts as a great creative force of the future, and when he became involved in the *Deutsche Werkbund*, the forerunner of the Bauhaus, he carried this educational concept with him. Finally, the Bauhaus itself was organized under the guidance of Walter Groupius in 1919, and moved through many experimental years until it closed in 1933 because of political problems caused by Hitler's accession to power in Germany.

At that time, and for a few years before, the teachers and students began to leave Germany and headed for the United States. Here in this country, their ideologies and philosophic aims continued to affect design and handicrafts. The Black

Mountain College in North Carolina became a center for many of these German refugees, and at Black Mountain students and faculty worked with such craftsmen/potters as Hamada from Japan, Bernard Leach from England, and Margarite Wildenheim of the United States. By the 1950s Black Mountain had fallen into various difficulties and lost its influence, but it had already left a deep impression on the arts within this country before closing in 1956.

While the Bauhaus was a school which only indirectly touched the life of Eaton, an organization that was to play a continued role in his life and in the development of handicrafts in this country was Pi Beta Phi. In 1912, Pi Beta Phi, a national sorority, established a small settlement school in Gatlinburg, Tennessee, to bring educational aid to the mountain families of the Smoky Mountain's surrounding villages. The school began with 10 children, and through continued support from Pi Beta Phi, today is a full community-supported public elementary school located on property which was donated by Pi Beta Phi to the city of Gatlinburg.

Throughout the development of the school, a health center was supported by federal and state funds with matching funds from Pi Beta Phi. But most important, Pi Beta Phi encouraged handicrafts production by the mountain people. The inhabitants of the area were encouraged to reawaken their traditional handicrafts, selling them eventually through the Arrowcraft Shop in Gatlinburg as an income-earning activity. The sale of handicrafts made by the mountain folk was more than a project located in Gatlinburg, however, for the members of Pi Beta Phi sold these handmade objects throughout the country in annual Christmas sales and at small individual gatherings, with the profits going into the development of crafts education.

The Pi Beta Phi settlement school moved from being a small institution which educated mountain children, provided health services, and kept alive mountain crafts, to a craft center of national and international fame, training hundreds of professional and non-professional craftsmen. Today, Arrowmont School of Arts and Crafts has a reputation of being a school founded on strong traditional educational philosophies, a crafts center experimenting in innovative teaching methods.

For several years Eaton taught a course in craft and art appreciation at Arrowmont. In a letter to Marian G. Heard, the first director of Arrowmont, dated February 3, 1951, he wrote, "If I ever get a few days off, I will try to let you know how very much the association with the workshop, with you and our dear associates has meant to me, so much that I must leave it largely to your imagination—but it will always be one of my greatest privileges. Remember me to each one as you can." While most of Eaton's association with Arrowmont took place in his later years, he left a strong impression there among the school's officials and its students.

Most of Eaton's first years at the Russell Sage Foundation were associated with his social welfare concerns, and during these years the handicrafts world crept lamely along without any significant leader, except in isolated areas like the Pi Beta Phi project, some rural development programs, and small contributions by varying educational programs in various universities. Eaton's main thrust was to begin in the 1930s.

Eaton concerned himself with many projects throughout his tenure with the Russell Sage Foundation. One which was a vanguard in the field of art education was his project with Henry Schaefer-Simmern, a man who would influence the discipline for many years to come.

It was not surprising that Eaton should meet Schaefer-Simmern after his arrival in this country from his native Germany, for Eaton was deeply involved in the immigrant programs of New York. Exactly how Eaton met him is unclear, but they did meet and developed a close relationship.

Schaefer-Simmern brought with him from Germany his documents and photographs illustrating "some remarkable results in creative drawing, painting and sculpture done by unschooled adults in Germany", which Eaton pointed out in his May 18, 1944, report to the Foundation Trustees. Eaton was very impressed with what he saw, and though research of this nature was not completely new in the field of art education, it was new to Eaton. Eaton was certainly not uninformed about various developments in art in the United States, but his deep interest in craft and art development from a social viewpoint probably kept him from reading a great deal of the new art education literature which was being published at this time. Gustav Britsch's book *Theorie Der Bildenden Kunst* had been published in 1926, and the year in which Eaton became involved with Schaefer-Simmern, 1939, Viktor Lowenfeld had published *The Nature of Creative Activity* in London.

In any case, Eaton could see the social value of Schaefer-Simmern's work. He immediately applied to the Foundation for financial aid for a project which would eventually lead to the publishing of Schaefer-Simmern's book *The Unfolding of Artistic Activity*, one of the most significant books in art education, which fit the Foundation's scope as:

Art Education as a Social Problem

On the basic understanding that an individual's creative work is of far greater value to him in his mental and emotional development than any second-hand or trained knowledge, and with the view of producing works of art in the way folk art is created, I established in 1929 by order of the City of Frankfort-on-Main, a special night school for unemployed workmen and laymen. The purpose of this school was to awaken the creative power which nature has given to every normal human being, by helping to unfold and develop the pictorial ability of this group of people through the particular medium of art. This means helping the individual to develop the ability to conceive and to put into concrete form his own image of the visible world.

To accomplish this purpose it was first of all necessary to determine the interests of these people, and to have them put down their own visual conception of their environment. By expressing this conception in a pictorial representation of their own conceptional world—or in other words, they were experiencing self-expression.

From very primitive beginnings, these unemployed were able to create within a short time simple works which closely resembled folk and peasant art as well as early works of art from early epochs. But the educational intent was not to create art in a general sense, as artistic perception and creative activity cannot be induced from within but must be experienced and won in its own way from within. Therefore, the problem was not at all to work off "art" on these people, but to develop their latent mental and emotional power. The one and only problem was to wake up in these socially suffering men a new power, to show them the reality of this power, and to give them again a spiritual existence in the knowledge that they were capable of taking part in all the creative processes of culture and mental form of all art. Creative work was considered not only a question of art, but a socially important matter and general pedagogical problem, a matter of social justice.

I shall not enlarge further on the results of this work other than to say that about sixty percent of these people were able to produce their own works—each following his own way in development. I have with me photographs of their works and many of the original drawings, which I believe speak for *themselves far better that I can. Of the remainder, thirty-five per cent dropped out of the school because of re-employment.*

To realize these educational ideas in this country, it was felt that from a sociological viewpoint, it would be valuable to include with a small group of unemployed two other groups—prisoners and seamen. Mr. and Mrs. Simkhovitch have expressed interest in my work to the point of offering a course for a few unemployed workmen and women in the setting of Greenwich House. The contact with the prisoners would be made through your Foundation, while the seamen's group could be formed through the Home for Old Seamen on Staten Island. Should we care to include a fourth group-type, the director of the Pratt Institute of Art has kindly offered the use of studios without charge.

The initial costs of this experiment would be small. To begin with I would only need paper, pencils, crayons, water-colors and brushes. Later on, I would need plaster of Paris, a few boards of wood, linen and wool for embroideries.

I am free to begin work at once and could devote my whole time or any fraction of it that you might desire. I would agree to write up the work as it progresses, noting all social, psychological and artistic implications, with the viewpoint of proving that Art Education in this sense is a new approach to social education in line with modern and progressive education.

Schaefer-Simmern's statement on art education as a social problem was included with Eaton's proposal of May 16, 1939, to the Foundation. In Eaton's proposal, he outlined factors which would be limitations placed upon Schaefer-Simmern by the Foundation.

Professor Schaefer-Simmern feels that if he had an opportunity to continue this work for one year he would, or he could have an excellent basis for a significant report. I believe this could be done under such a plan as we have discussed and I therefore recommend the undertaking and suggest that we take immediate steps to get it under way.

I suggest, and this I believe to be in accordance with Professor Schaefer-Simmern's wishes that we count upon his giving not less than half or more than two thirds time to the work, and that it be under our direction and in accordance with a plan as carefully thought out as we can make it, but leaving room for such modification as may seem desirable as we proceed. In addition to conducting the classes and keeping records, we would wish him to do some research in the literature, especially of Germany, on this subject to aid in developing a philosophy which might be needed in case of publication. Of course very careful written case records would accompany the teaching . . .

The honorarium which Professor Schaefer-Simmern and I have discussed is $50 to $60 per month, and perhaps $100 for tools and materials, which he may use, and for unforeseen expenses . . . I have also made it clear that I would assume responsibility for directing the undertaking for the Foundation. The Foundation would also have the first claim upon the results of the experiment for publication in case we desired to use it in this way, but of course Professor Schaefer-Simmern would be given credit for the work done.

The project was approved and started in July 1939. It was apparently a success as far as Eaton and the Foundation were concerned. Although Eaton does not mention it in his personal correspondence as he did with much of the work in which he was involved, he again mentioned the work in a memo to Harrison, his immediate supervisor, on January 26, 1942, under the heading of *Experimental Studies in Arts and Crafts*:

> *The experiments in creative expression carried on by Professor Schaefer-Simmern during the past two years among untrained adults, immigrant groups, seamen, and young men in a reformatory have been demonstrated through a series of exhibitions of the works of each individual. The plan for continuing these experiments, or similar ones, is as yet undetermined, but discussions are underway for perhaps an enlarged program to be carried out by Professor Schaefer-Simmern under the direction of the Department, and a record of the experiment published in some form.*

By 1943, the Board of Trustees of the Foundation was attempting to force Eaton into retirement. Eaton was very sensitive about the retirement rules at the Foundation; moreover he was concerned about the many projects he had on the drawing board and not yet completed. The biggest of these projects was the study and investigation of the handicrafts of New England. He was still very much at work on the final publication, and felt it was just not possible to retire at this time. Added to this were several other major projects of his, plus the Schaefer-Simmern work. Through many letters of appeals and reports to the Trustees, he managed to remain at the Foundation until 1946, when he was 68 years of age. Throughout this time period, he continued to work with Schaefer-Simmern, but by 1944, funds were cut, probably because the Foundation wanted to ease Eaton out of his responsibilities. In *The Russell Sage Foundation 1907-1946* published in 1947, the authors Glenn, Brandt, and Andrews state that the Schaefer-Simmern project was completed in 1944 and that the results were to be published by another publishing house.

Schaefer-Simmern's book *The Unfolding of Artistic Activity* eventually was published by University of California Press in 1948, rather than by Russell Sage Foundation. There is no question that his work has generated many discussions within the field of art education. The book is still used as a resource in art education research.

While it cannot be said that Eaton was completely responsible for Schaefer-Simmern's work being conducted, it is safe to assume that Eaton's interest in the work did help to move the research toward an earlier realization. Eaton as a social researcher concerned himself with the problems of this country's social development and its relationship to art. Through his determination, he was able to bring about a new look in the investigation of art. His work with Schaefer-Simmern was only a small part of the projects he innovatively led, while he tried to understand and assist the social and cultural growth of ethnic minority groups. The Russell Sage Foundation gave him the platform to realize the marrying of the arts and crafts to social problems.

Immigrant Gifts To American Life

"There is no danger I think that we cannot Americanize our immigrants; the danger is rather that in the process we may overlook and lose some of the best elements which we need in the building of our national life.

Allen Eaton—*Immigrant Gifts to American Life*

Yugoslavian string orchestra and singers at the Buffalo Art and Crafts Exhibition. *Photo from* Immigrant Gifts to American Life.

E aton's interest and concern for immigrants was deep, for he understood their relationship with the development of our country. In his youth, he had seen first-hand the Oriental immigrants on the West Coast, and watched their cultures weave into the rich fabric of the American people. Now, living in the East, he became very aware of the valid and important contributions immigrants there were making through introducing their artistic and cultural talents to the United States.

The residue of the discrimination he had experienced in Oregon was still there, and continued to be apparent through the 1920s in many of his contacts and associations with Oregonians and past Oregonians living in the East, but even so he was an ardent advocate of the University. On June 5, 1924, he wrote to Eric Allen at the University of Oregon concerning his activities in helping alumni collect contributions for the University. "I came across one person who said he would have nothing to do with a matter with a pro-German in charge. This for a minute broke me in two. Then it flashed upon me that the people at home would probably think I had not raised anything because of the same thing."

Eaton was very alert to the fact that immigrants also were discriminated against, and that few people could see any value in their lifestyles and cultural patterns. Eaton points out in his author's preface to *Immigrant Gifts to American Life* that while "we spend millions of dollars annually in our schools to teach foreign languages to American-born children, is it not absurd that we object to those who teach their mother tongue to their American-born children in their homes and societies?" His attempt then was to bridge the gap of understanding between those who were new to the nation and those who were old residents.

Eaton started his work with immigrants through the auspices of the American Federation of Arts, the University of the State of New York, and the City of Buffalo. While this involvement began before he accepted the position with the

Russell Sage Foundation, he continued to work on this project for many years.

On May 18, 1944, Eaton outlined some of his work during the years with the Foundation and informally discussed them with the Trustees in order to obtain a stay from forced retirement at the age of 65. In his outline for this meeting, he talks about his work with immigrants using words which he had used before in previous communications to the Trustees.

> *The work with the Emergency Fleet Corporation, which was a part of the U.S. Shipping Board, was the prevention of strikes and lockouts and their earliest possible adjustment when they did occur in New York, New Jersey, and part of New England, for then as today, the great job was to keep production going on the home front (in World War I). This work brought me in continuous touch with countless foreign citizens, many of whom could not speak our language, but who like their sons and brothers in the armed service had the spirit of Americanism in their hearts and the will to make any sacrifice. Many of these workers in the war plants revealed, often through interpreters, some of the finest human qualities and a loyalty to America which I could never forget. And often I could see backgrounds and cultural traditions of great value among these immigrants.*

> *Yet because they were so handicapped in speech and in writing, and many had not been able to gain an economic foothold here, they were often unable to make themselves understood to their employers, and their real traits and qualities were often unrecognized, and their cultural backgrounds and the best traditions unappreciated. Before the war (World War I) ended I resolved that, if I ever could find any way to do so, I would try to do something*

to help interpret these immigrants to our native born citizens, and reciprocally our native born citizens to them.

This opportunity came when Mr. De Forest, as President of the American Federation of Arts, asked me to tell him, as he puts it, 'a way or two,' in which this national art organization could be vitally related to the everyday life of the American people. The war had ended, and our nation was embarking upon a rather intensive campaign of Americanization in which many people were telling our immigrant citizens and prospective citizens what the country had done for them, and adding, in some instances, that if they didn't like our constitution and our ways of living that they should go back to the country that they came from. This method of Americanization was not helping the Americans who were forming classes for immigrants, and helping them gain their American citizenship.

In answer to Mr. De Forest's question I suggested that the American Federation of Arts, in cooperation with other agencies, strike a new note in Americanization—that instead of telling the immigrant what America had done for him, that we proclaim publicly what the immigrant had done for America; and, when Mr. De Forest asked how this could be done through the arts, I outlined a program of community projects to be based upon local exhibitions of Arts and Crafts of the Homelands of Europe. These exhibitions to be held in the principal cities of New York State first, if we could get the full cooperation of the State Department of Education. This cooperation we did get through Dr. John Finley who was then Commissioner of Education for the State of New York.

> *As a matter of fact, all of these New York State projects were carried out under the auspices of the State and Local Boards of Education—including the ones known as 'America's Making,' which were held in New York City. These exhibitions, the first to take place in our country, were held in Buffalo, Albany, Rochester, and finally New York City. The Buffalo and Albany exhibitions I installed and directed, and helped in the planning of those in Rochester and New York. In each of these, native and foreign-born citizens joined in exhibits, pageants, entertainment programs, addresses, and the printed page to set forth contributions of our foreign-born citizens to American life and culture. The Foundation later considered these events important enough to record and build upon . . .*

The book *Immigrant Gifts to American Life* was the result of the various exhibitions of handicrafts which were held initially in New York State. After the first exhibitions were held in Buffalo, Albany, and Rochester, many other communities along the eastern seaboard took up the interest in such activities which would bring about a closer connection between immigrants and "old Americans." As each one was held, Eaton was determined to include a report of the display of handicrafts in his planned Russell Sage publication. From the exhibition in Buffalo, October 22, 1919, until 1932, when the Folk Council of New York gave two programs at the Guild Theatre, he was constantly revising and adding to the publication.

The delay in publication came not only from his intense interest in having a complete record of these immigrant activities, but also from his many tasks within the Russell Sage Foundation which held him back to some extent. The *Arts and Crafts of the Homelands* report, which was to be financed and published by the Foundation, was planned to act as the catalog of the Buffalo exhibition. In the *Art Catalog and Yearbook 1920*

Norwegian, Danish and Swedish exhibit at the Art and Crafts of the Homeland Exhibition *in the Albright Art Gallery, Buffalo, New York. Photo from* Immigrant Gifts to American Life.

of the Buffalo Fine Arts Academy, the art director points out that, "No catalogue was printed by the Academy for the Exhibition of *Arts and Crafts of the Homelands,*" although in the *Academy Notes,* Vol. 15, 1920, there is a small article about the show. It therefore was important for Eaton eventually to make sure his work was reported in full.

Even though there was no catalog, Eaton recorded each piece with love as the immigrants brought in their beloved possessions for exhibition. He had placed announcements in local Buffalo newspapers, and sent word to the various clubs and societies of the different nationalities. The response was tremendous, and Eaton just could not bear to turn anyone away. He was especially pleased that different groups wanted to perform at the exhibit, so vocal groups as well as small instrumental groups were invited to play a part in making the exhibition a total story of the arts from across the ocean.

Like all of the books he was to write in later years, his *Immigrant Gifts to American Life* was painstakingly put together until it suited him perfectly.

Of all the reviews which came out covering the book's 1932 publication, the one which had the most meaning for Eaton was that written by his friend Ellis F. Lawrence, Dean and Director of the School of Fine Arts at the University of Oregon. The review was published in the October 15, 1932, issue of the *Portland Spectator*, and highly praised the new book. Lawrence carefully took each chapter and reported its contents along with various quotations from the material itself. One quote which Lawrence made from the book expresses Eaton's philosophy that all people can create beautiful things, whether they are highly trained or simple craftsmen:

> *It is not the thing which is done that makes a work of art, it is the manner of doing it. These exhibitions of things made by unschooled but sensitive people who knew not the rules of composition and color, but who felt strongly the impulse to create beautiful objects and responded to that impulse, will not only help us to appreciate more fully the folk culture of the many homelands from which America is made up, but they will give us a vision of what we may reasonably hope to see in a renaissance of all the arts in our country. Perhaps the greatest thing, however, they will do is to*

Swedish immigrant's trunk at the Buffalo Art and Crafts Exhibition, *1793 & 1805. Photo from* Immigrant Gifts to American Life.

help us understand that art in its true sense, whether it be folk or fine, is the expression of joy in work.

Lawrence was one of the few reviewers of Eaton's work who did not recall Eaton's expulsion from Oregon as a part of his review. Yet even he was compelled to make a side comment at the very end of his review which related directly to Eaton's past in a very subtle and quiet way. The last two paragraphs were devoted to this story:

> *A few months ago on a train on the Sante Fe, the reviewer found himself in an improvised bridge game. His partner proved to be a former Oregonian. When he learned the residence of the reviewer, he remarked: 'Ah, that's a state for you: How I love it! I'd go back there to die but they drove me out. They didn't want my service.'*

> "Too many native and adopted sons of Oregon have left the state. We would do well to consider

why! But at least we can do ourselves the honor of recognizing their achievements in other fields and perhaps we can, by so doing, learn better how to make use of those who see fit to remain Oregonians, in residence.

Soon after *Immigrant Gifts* was published, Eaton wrote an article for the February 1933 issue of *School Arts* magazine. Called "Immigrant Arts in America", it was less about art than about the need to understand immigrants and immigration. His deep interest in immigrants and discrimination almost makes us think that he too felt as though he were an immigrant. He understood their problems of being uprooted from their homelands, facing adversity, and attempting to find new directions for their lives. But regardless what problems he had, in his soft and gentle manner, he still easily forgot and forgave, and in this article, he speaks of tolerance as though he had never had any problems. "Nothing becomes us better or reflects more truly that spirit of tolerance which has long been one of our proud traditions than our joining with native and foreign born citizens in appreciation of their contributions to American culture which have come to us through our immigrant citizens from across the sea."

Eaton remembered the persecution of the Japanese and Chinese in the West; and even though United States newspapers consistently raved about the waves of arriving immigrants, and even though he saw the problems of the Japanese-Americans during World War II, Eaton was able to look without hate on the problem and work toward bridging the gap. His innocence, and, at times naiveté, certainly showed through, but the end result was a man who loved people and always saw the best in them. Marian Heard described him as a "gentle, kind and warm man. One whom you wanted to take care of and watch over to make sure nothing happened to him." This was a far different man from the descriptions of him during his legislature days in Oregon.

Polish, Hungarian and German booths at the Homelands Exhibit *held in the State Museum at Trenton, New Jersey. Photo from* Immigrant Gifts to American Life.

The *Arts and Crafts of the Homeland Exhibit* ushered Eaton into the position of being one of, if not the only, experts in the field of handicrafts in the United States. With the background of his work in the 1920s he stepped into the 1930s and into the major work of his life. He was now involved in an area of specialization which would earn him the title of Dean of American Crafts.

In the Russell Sage Foundation history, written by Glenn, Brandt, and Andrews, the effects of *Immigrant Gifts to American Life* are beautifully listed.

> *The book ran through two printings; before it finally went out of print in 1944, much evidence accumulated in its varied uses and wide influence. It was an aid in citizenship courses in schools and colleges. It stimulated many exhibits, festivals, and special occasions featuring the contributions of immigrants to American culture; examples were a Fourth of July pageant of foreign-born citizens at*

Oglebay Park, Wheeling, West Virginia, and a long series of Festival of Nations in St. Paul, Minnesota. As time went on, the Department was called upon for increasing service in this field, sometimes more than it was able to render in view of other commitments. Its report for 1939, after indicating the necessity for many refusals, nevertheless includes a record of Mr. Eaton's services in suggesting materials and other ideas for the national Folk Festival, Washington, D.C.; the Folk Festival, St. Paul, Minnesota; folk festivals at the New York World's Fair; the Service Bureau for International Education; a teaching unit on races and nationalities in the New York public schools; the Hall of Nations of the American University Graduate School, Washington, D.C.; the Immigration and Naturalization Service, Ellis Island; a New York City conference on the immigrant and the community. The Federal Office of Education broadcasts entitled 'Americans All-Immigrants' used extensive quotations and materials from Immigrant Gifts to American Life.

During that and the following year Mr. Eaton served as a member of the American Common committee of the New York World's Fair, which arranged the Hall of Fame at the American Common, stressing contributions from the foreign born, and planned the nationality programs given at the Fair.

Handicrafts Of The Southern Highlands

Like Thomas Wolfe, I "look homeward seeing the faces of Appalachia. The Real people of the 1930s discovered in their fair deal, square deal, government of the people by the people of social consciousness, TVA, welfare and 'social security'."

Charles Counts

George McCarter, noted basket maker, April 5, 1939. Courtesy of Arrowmont School of Arts and Crafts.

Allen Eaton's entrance into the world of the Southern Highlands was the beginning of what was to become his most important work. It was through his constant concern with the handicrafts of the Highlands that his fame grew and the importance of handicraft development emerged as a significant part of American life. His work in North Carolina, Tennessee, Virginia, and Kentucky brought him everlasting friendships and a deep love for the Appalachian Mountains. There is hardly a village or craft settlement or craftsman in the area who was not touched, in some manner, by the thoughts and ideas of Eaton.

Bernice Stevens tells of a trip which she and several friends made into Georgia. "There was a man by the name of Meaders, a potter, in Georgia. While Mr. Eaton was still living, we happened to be going by the pottery and because I had never seen it, or met Mr. Meaders, we stopped and made ourselves known. In order to establish some kind of relationship with Meaders, we mentioned several people we knew and also Eaton. After that he could talk about no one except Eaton. He said, 'You just write Allen Eaton and tell him it has been too long since he has been down here and for him to come back and see me.' And so many of the people who were just country craftsmen—uneducated. They just thought Eaton was God."

Eaton first came to the Southern Highlands in 1926 with Olive Dame Campbell of the Campbell Folk School to attend a conference of the Southern Mountain Workers. It was the first time this organization had the topic of handicrafts on the agenda. This led to an informal meeting of a group of craftspeople in December 1928 at Penland, North Carolina.

Penland was to become of national importance in future years as an educational craft center, but when Miss Lucy Morgan first established the Penland Weavers in 1923, it was far off in the mountains, and unknown to most of the country. However, it slowly was built into a very fine school by Miss Morgan, and by 1929 was called the Penland School of Handicrafts. Today its name is Penland School of Crafts. Like Arrowmont Arts and

Crafts School in Gatlinburg, Tennessee, and Haystack School of Crafts at Deer Isle, Maine, it draws students from around the world, and has an exceptionally fine faculty.

When Miss Morgan invited the group to meet at Penland, she was sure they would refuse. In her book *Gift from the Hills*, she writes how excited she was that her invitation was accepted. Eaton was the first to arrive. "I took my little Ford to meet him at Penland Station and as we drove around our snowy curves to ascend the steep slope, my senses were alert for a tenseness, an anxiety, a pressing of the floor boards by Mr. Eaton. But even as we rounded the Big Turn and the back wheels slithered toward the outer edge of the road, Mr. Eaton seemed as relaxed and calm and happy as if he had been riding these hills every day. In fact, he seemed more composed than I actually felt."

In 1954, Eaton returned to Penland for the 25th anniversary of the school. Miss Morgan again remarks about Eaton:

> *But of all our anniversary visitors, none brought us more joy in coming to see us, I'm sure, than a beloved friend of many years who was coming to a Penland he had done so much to help set on its course, Mr. Allen Eaton, author of* Handicrafts of the Southern Highlands. *I think of him as a guiding star in the days when the Southern Highland Handicraft Guild was making its way through its period of growing pains and joys.*

At the December 1928 meeting he came as a representative of the Russell Sage Foundation, and Mrs. Campbell had suggested to the group that Eaton be at the meeting as an advisor. But according to Clementine Douglas, the decision to organize into the Southern Highlands Handicrafts Guild was made at the December 28, 1929, meeting in her shop, which Eaton also attended. At this meeting, held at the Spinning Wheel, in Asheville, North Carolina, there were many people

Gatlinburg, Tennessee Fair, Pi Beta Phi School, October 13, 1923.
Courtesy of Arrowmont School of Arts and Crafts.

who felt the need to bring about an organization that could
unite the Southern Highland craftsmen. Among these people
were Helen Dingman of Berea, Kentucky; Frances Goodrich of
Allanstand; Lucy Morgan of Penland; Evelyn Bishop of Pi Beta
Phi; Olive Dame Campbell and Louise Pitman of the Campbell
Folk School. Also in attendance were Dr. Mary Sloop of the
Crossmore School; Wilmer Stone of the Saluda Weavers; and
Clementine Douglas. Clem, as Miss Douglas was known, was
always pleased to think that this organization was started in her
simple shop, and often told Louise Pitman, her best friend,
"What a joy it is to me to think back on those days when we
organized right here on the Spinning Wheel."

Eaton's presence at these meetings was to be the beginning
of not only a long association with the Southern Highlands, but
also a close and deep personal relationship with Clem.

But to some of the older members of the Southern Highland
Handicraft Guild, the meeting at the Spinning Wheel was not
the one which formally organized or established the Guild.
According to Louise Pitman, at the first meeting in December
1928, they discussed various problems of sales, the marketing
of handicrafts, and the goal of obtaining some technical assistance and a specialist.

*That must be the gist of what they discussed in
1928. Then I think it was picked up and there was
discussion of a conference meeting in Knoxville in
1929. Then there was another meeting, held in the
old Spinning Wheel, in December 1929, a year after
the Penland one. And that was when they voted to
organize—and this is a point of contention, because
Clem used to say that the Guild was formed right
there in her Spinning Wheel. Well. It really wasn't. It
was the Spring of 1930 at the conference in Knoxville
when we adopted by-laws and really became an
organization.*

O.J. Mattil, a cabinetmaker of Gatlinburg, Tennessee, and
Marian Heard of Arrowmont both felt that without the aid of
Eaton, the Guild would never have organized; however, Louise
Pitman feels that it just would have taken a much longer time.

When Eaton returned to New York, apparently after and
from the December 1928 meeting in Penland, he prepared a
long memo to Shelby Harrison recommending that further work
be directed toward the handicrafts in the Southern Highlands.
The memo was dated October 23, 1929, which was before the
Spinning Wheel meeting, but after the Penland meeting.

The subject of The Arts and Crafts in American
Homes *is very comprehensive and may seem to cover
too large an area for an initial undertaking, but it will
lend itself to smaller units which can be complete in
themselves and each of which will contribute to the
larger subject. It would seem to me better to choose
an inclusive subject and then develop parts of it as
intensively as seems justified. For instance, within
the scope of* The Arts and Crafts in American Homes,
a study of the Fireside Industries of the Southern
Highlands *would fit perfectly and would probably
prove sufficiently important to justify the publication*

of an early and separate report. In any case it would enable us to secure for the handicraft workers of that region some of the facts which they have asked for and which they need as a basis for the development of the handicrafts association they are now forming. There is no area in our country where the handicrafts are more widely practiced and no place where they have a greater social and economic significance. The output of handicrafts of the Southern Highlands measured in terms of dollars probably exceeds that of any other area on the continent, unless it be the Province of Quebec.

If we should choose the Southern Highlands area for the first, much of the first material to be gathered would be through correspondence and conference with mountain leaders with whom we are in touch.

While I have not recently given the matter of procedure much thought, I would think the procedure might be as follows:

1. As complete a list as possible should be made of the handicraft centers in the Southern Highlands and a preliminary map filled in to show the relative location . . .

2. Some basic information should be gathered by mail as to what these different centers are doing . . .

3. The association of those interested in the handicrafts will probably hold a meeting in the near future when it should be possible to get from them a statement of the information they need most in promoting the practice of the handicrafts. Their need was roughly covered in the Penland Conference notes.

Other points were also listed in Eaton's memo to Harrison, the bulk relating to work with the Department of Agriculture and the Bureau of Education. Each of the areas he stressed was aimed at reaching a closer relationship between the arts and social sciences. Eaton was very interested in the arts of country life, the influence of beauty in the lives of working people, the therapeutic value of art, and the value of arts and crafts in adult education and the public schools.

The Southern Highlands Handicraft Guild grew rapidly, holding meetings in various parts of the Appalachians. In one of Clem Douglas' speeches, she defined the purposes of the Guild in simple terms: "The purposes behind this cooperative enterprise are three—economic, aesthetic, and social; its aim, to fill the three-fold need of man for Bread, Beauty, and Brotherhood." Today, the Guild's central offices are in Asheville, North Carolina at the Folk Art Center on the Blue Ridge Parkway with Ruth T. Summers as Executive Director.

The Guild participated in many activities in its formative years. Eaton often encouraged the Guild to take important leadership in these activities. In 1933, the American Country Life Association held a large exhibition in Blacksburg, Virginia, of handicrafts which the Guild collected. After the show in Blacksburg, the collection circulated throughout the country. The first summer Guild Fair, however, was not held until 1948.

Eaton became a frequent visitor to the Southern Highlands region. His list of friends multiplied and his fame spread throughout the mountains, and as his fame spread, he slowly became known as the "AE of the Southern Highlands." By the late thirties AE was a well-established name for Eaton. In many articles about him, and in many letters, the initials AE are used rather than Allen Eaton. This new nickname for him came through the Irish poet-painter George William Russell.

Russell who was born in Armagh, Ireland, in 1867, became very involved in agricultural cooperatives in addition to his

Unidentified mountain craftsman. Courtesy of Arrowmont School of Arts and Crafts.

poetic and artistic pursuits. Russell came to the United States for the first time in 1928, and managed to befriend many famous people during his stay. Al Smith, Governor of New York, and Colonel House, President Woodrow Wilson's right-hand man, were among those he met. Russell came to this country under the auspices of the Department of Agriculture and lectured throughout the United States on agricultural foundations and rural cooperatives. Russell's book *National Being* was well-known in this country, especially the rural aspects of the publication. Russell felt very much at home in the Southern states, and traveled extensively throughout the same area in which Eaton was working. Russell used the initials AE from a very early time in his writing and painting. He had decided to title a painting *Birth of Aeon* after he had heard whispers in the winds suggesting this title. Later he signed his writings "Aeon," but through a printer's mistake, "Aeon" was changed to "AE". From then on Russell began using AE.

Since to some of the people of the Southern Highlands Eaton reflected so much of the poetry of Russell (AE), and since he also traveled throughout the country attempting to help rural people, he also became AE. Exactly who coined this nickname is unknown, but it is fairly sure that the name probably came from Clem Douglas and Louise Pitman.

From the time Eaton became involved in the activities of the handicrafts of the Southern Highlands, he began to accumulate his material for the Russell Sage Foundation report. He traveled constantly throughout the Southern states, usually with Clem Douglas as his companion. Slowly the stories and mythology about Eaton grew—each person that he met was able to tell a new story about Allen Eaton and what kind of person he was. Few people could remember any unfavorable stories. He worked with individuals living in isolated log cabins, he lectured groups of diligent craftsmen, and he gathered the handicrafts of the region for exhibitions and displays. During the years from 1930 until his book *Handicrafts of the Southern Highlands* was published by the Foundation in 1937, he also wrote many articles about the handicrafts and attended many and various conferences concerning the enrichment of rural life.

Eaton was a woodsman. He loved to saw wood, and he enjoyed trees and woodpiles. Eaton was very unpretentious, and he identified with the common people. Undoubtedly this is why his book about handicrafts reflected the people about whom he wrote. Year after year, he wrote in his Christmas letters about the saga of a beech tree which grew on his property, but caused him undue anxiety, as we will see later. This very common down-to-earth story, along with his other attitudes, gave him the aura of a country philosopher. Throughout his Christmas letter of 1931, when he was deep into his survey of handicrafts of the Southern Highlands, he wrote about sawing wood.

> *That for one born and raised in the country, as I have been, there is a satisfaction about getting in one's own winter wood which passeth understanding. It is not only that by so doing he is thrice warmed by the same wood, once in the forest, then at his wood pile, and finally at the family fireplace, a wonderful economy which too few men can indulge in; but in the whole process there is a rare blend of physical and intellectual recreation which I cannot commend too highly. From the first strike of the ax to the final push of the saw or swing of the sledge there is a healthful exercise for muscles, lungs and heart and this is all the more pleasurable because of its close association with nature, especially in these first stages of the work done in the woods. After the plan for cutting the trees has been roughly laid out then there is more time for mental relaxation. Much of the work takes on a rhythm and into its swing anticipations of crisp winter nights around the hearth with family, friends, and books, not to mention pippins and cheese, popcorn and cider, and nuts from Uncle George's.*

Then as the old crosscut saw swings back and forth
settling slowly into the heart of the wood memories
are stirred running back through childhood to father
and mother and grandparents and pioneer neighbors
at the other end of the Oregon Trail.

Bernice Stevens commented that "he felt one of the most beautiful things in the world was a woodpile. I never see a woodpile that I don't think of Eaton. My friend Zim and I always think 'AE should see that.'"

His daughter Elizabeth felt, "These letters are not important. They do not reflect the man. Just an attempt of a very tired 'woodsman' at a bit of drollery when and if it occurred." His Appalachian friends, however, felt differently about the annual Christmas letter, and it seems that each person saved a few of the letters throughout the years. While the letters did not seem to impress his family, they related very much to the people in the mountains, because he too was a common man, as they were always quick to point out. They accepted him because of his down-home philosophy. He was not a New Yorker there to tell them what to do about their world.

When he traveled around he often stayed with the craftspeople in their mountain log cabins. Louise Pitman tells a story of one of his visits to a local log cabin where he spent the night. "Well, now I can tell you of one tale. There is this picture in this book (*Southern Highlands*). A lovely cabin, where I spent many a night, and we went there from the Folk School with a friend. Fisher, a woodworker went with us. They slept up in the attic and I slept in that attic many a times. The Wilson family lived there and they had quilts hung all over the walls to keep it warm. And Fisher, who was with AE said, 'In the middle of the night I woke up, and there he was—he had candles and he was going around studying the stitches on the quilts.' He just loved it. He really did."

This kind of behavior on Eaton's part endeared him to the people, and they listened to him carefully because they were well aware that he understood handicrafts and the manner in which they were created. A craftswoman who responded directly to Eaton's encouragement was Granny Donaldson. Marian Heard tells about Granny Donaldson and the cow blankets.

When he was writing the book on crafts of the Southern Highlands, he went to the John C. Campbell School in order to engender enthusiasm in the crafts—to open them up. He brought along a whole lot of goodies from his home to show them crafts were being made in other countries. He brought among other things, a cow blanket from Italy, and he explained—and they got in all these country folks from around Brasstown—and he explained how in other countries like Italy they put cow designs on blankets. Well, Granny Donaldson was cooking for the Campbell Folk School, and she went home that night and on just a piece of plain unbleached muslin, she whipped up or crocheted these animals. And when she came in the next morning, she brought this cow blanket for Eaton to see. These were always referred to as Granny Donaldson's cow blankets. They are collectors' items now and we have two here at Arrowmont. It got so people would weave backgrounds for these. She was about 95 when she did this, and until her death that was her income— making Granny Donaldson cow blankets.

Louise Pitman had provided the first background fabric for her along with the yarns. Eaton inspired many people to begin handicrafts. Each little community has a story to tell about his visit and how he had excited them into working.

Eaton never brought his family with him when he came to the Southern Highlands, and so Clem became his surrogate family.

Granny Donaldson with crocheted cow blanket.
Courtesy of Arrowmont School of Arts and Crafts.

Clementine Douglas was born in Jacksonville, Florida, on December 27, 1893; a great deal of her early life was spent traveling from Florida to the Northeast, where Clem had been taken to a Boston hospital for medical care when she was a child. She attended a boarding school in Connecticut when 16, and following that she was sent to Holton Arms School in Washington, D.C. Her interests were in the arts, and for two years she studied at Pratt Institute in Brooklyn. By the summer of 1918 she was fairly well-steeped in art, but to some extent had not yet found her real calling.

She was introduced to the crafts of the Southern Highlands by Helen H. Dingman, an educator at Berea College, at a lecture Miss Dingman gave about the work she was doing in Kentucky. When Miss Dingman appealed for help with the mountain project, Clem was converted and volunteered her services. So in the summer of 1919, Clem went to Kentucky. There she immersed herself in working for three summers, until finally after a trip to Europe, and after having learned a great deal from her experience in Kentucky, she decided to establish a weaving studio in Asheville, North Carolina. In 1925, she found a hundred-year-old log cabin on top of a mountain near Asheville, and had it moved to a site that became her Spinning Wheel studio and shop.

She became a legend in the Southern Highlands, working constantly to further the handicrafts and the lives of the mountain craftspeople. In 1940, Clem moved her Spinning Wheel to another location, which had a small modern house behind it and a beautifully landscaped property. She remained there until her death, except for journeys to Haiti and other places where she worked on various crafts projects. In 1957, Clem added another small house to the property so that Louise Pitman, her dear friend, could have a home. They planned the place together and with a local carpenter built a charming house for Louise. It was to this small compound of buildings that Eaton came when he traveled through the Southern Highlands.

When Eaton was not with Clem traveling through the mountains or working on exhibitions, they kept up a flood of letters some very professional in nature, and, as the years passed, others very personal. Letters which he sent to her from his office at the Foundation were usually typed by his secretary Matilda Heidtman, and always were signed "Sincerely," while those he wrote in long-hand were signed "Affectionately". It was almost as though he carried on two separate streams of correspondence. Here are a few excerpts:

> July 24, 1934: *I do think the growing interest in the folk arts, of which the peasant arts are a part and all of which are really related to the handicrafts of the highlands, might be a line that you could profitably do something with in connection with your own and other mountain things.*

> January 25, 1937: *Rural handicrafts I think are at the beginning of their development in our country.*

> September 25, 1942: *I am interested in your statements about keeping the quality or rather the standard of craftsmanship up in the therapeutic field as well as in others. Great advancement has been made in this respect since the last war, particularly in the general field of occupational therapy where some of the best work in the country is now being done. I think it would be a fine thing if you would arrange with someone to have a committee get in touch with the leaders in the therapeutic field. I know some of them and if you decide to do this I will be glad to send you a little later the names and addresses of the people who would not only be helpful to you but who would be very glad of your association.*

> November 1944: *I need the spiritual refreshment a visit with you would give me. How can we do it. Take good care of yourself Clem there is so much which you can do better than anybody. Affectionately, A.E.*

March 3, 1951: *I am crazy to know as much as possible about what you have been doing—are doing and how.*

Late in 1951: about the book *Beauty Behind Barbed Wire: This is the only book I have written which I feel every American should know about. It is a record of one of the most remarkable chapters in the history of the arts . . .The greatest betrayal of constitutional rights in our history.*

On July 20, 1952, he wrote from Eugene, Oregon, where he was visiting, concerning his despair at not being with her at the Asheville Fair, and in July 1954 he wrote: *The possibility of seeing you in July lifts my spirits high . . ."* He was preparing for a trip down to the Southern Highlands again.

On August 15, 1954, he wrote: *It was the great experience of looking backward and seeing how all our efforts have counted, and looking forward with full confidence that what we have done together has established a continuity which will continue into the long future enriching the lives of others as well as our own, and extending to countless deserving people that we—the pioneers—let us call ourselves among ourselves—will never know.*

January 1960 (from New Delhi, India): *The public part of this letter can proclaim from the house tops of the Southern Highlands and the United States that the* Handicraft Exhibition *in the first* World's Agricultural Fair *is a success and it is due first of all to the Southern Highlands Handicraft Guild.*

August 1962: *Dear Clem: It is just about that time in the morning when some time ago you brought to my bedside a warm drink that sustained me all the way to India and back and has continued to keep me going ever since.*

Their correspondence was considerable and ranged in topics from their pets to the latest in governmental craft developments. In March 1962, Eaton wrote to Clem after he had made a trip to Asheville. Although it was not the last letter that passed between them, Bernice Stevens of Gatlinburg, said that it was like a farewell letter.

> *I know the snow was beautiful, and thanks for your delightful account of your bird visitors—very real to me now that I know all the charming places (in your home and garden) and (I see) a hundred times and more the signs of spring coming out of your sacred ground especially the lovely clump of blue iris. I shouldn't be partial, for other blossoms were as beautiful, yet somehow they come into my mind oftenest, like a tiny yellow buttercup blossoming on the edge of the snow by our family spring in Oregon. I know I have thought of it ten thousand times—and each time it has made me happy—as the recollection of the iris will in all the days to come . . .Good night Clem. Thanks for everything . . .Bless you as you bless me.*

Many people watched the relationship of Eaton and Clem grow and blossom, each having different thoughts about the type of friendship it was. In a taped interview with Bernice Stevens, she elaborated on her thoughts.

> *I can't tell you for sure because I don't know. But I was always convinced that they were in love with each other. I don't think he and his wife were too close. Clem was just a different person when Allen was around. Of course, all the women around here in crafts loved Allen, because he did so much for the Guild. We all just felt he was wonderful, but he and Clem had a very special relationship. How far it went, or what type of relationship it was nobody*

knows. *But he stayed with her always when he went to Asheville, and they were just very close. And she gave him money when he needed it, and he always needed it. I know that she bailed him out more than once. When he would get low and want things, she would see that he got what he wanted. She sent him money when he went to India . . .to buy things. She was awfully good to him.*

Marian Heard said, "Clem and he were so close. When you saw them together they just enjoyed every minute. It made you sick to know what the situation was at home with him. I remember the time we were all taking a bus to Asheville to the Fair, but Mr. Eaton and Clem took Clem's car ahead of the bus. And somewhere as we went over the mountains, we came around the curve and there they were with a picnic blanket spread out—having lunch and wine. Just like two lovebirds."

Louise Pitman felt that they had a very close relationship, but one that was only platonic and that it probably could never have developed into any other kind of relationship.

⁕

The 1930s were busy years for Eaton. He traveled extensively throughout the United States, giving lectures, attending various handicraft meetings, and setting up different exhibitions. In 1932, he helped collect crafts for the American Country Life Association annual meeting in Blacksburg, Virginia. This exhibition was later circulated by the American Federation of Art to many national galleries. When the show first opened in Blacksburg, it was sponsored by Mrs. Calvin Coolidge, Mrs. Herbert Hoover, and Mrs. Franklin D. Roosevelt.

He was especially involved with agricultural extension services as he started to arrange for the *Rural Arts Exhibition* in Washington, D.C. This exhibition was sponsored in 1937 by the Department of Agriculture to celebrate its 75th anniversary and was the first of its kind in the United States. Clem, of course, came to help him select, set up displays, and to keep Eaton moving along. The Southern Highlands Handicraft Guild provided her with funds for this trip. Together they worked night and day in order to be ready for the grand opening on November 14, which was to attract top government officials plus hundreds of foreign dignitaries and guests.

It was during this exhibition that Eaton began a close friendship with Eleanor Roosevelt, and through many years after kept up a continuing correspondence with her concerning the arts in the United States. Eaton acted as her guide through the exhibition, and during their viewing of the handicrafts, Mrs. Roosevelt spied a lovely hand carved pig which had been made at the John C. Campbell Folk School. She was so pleased with it that she bought it for FDR. Legend says that when he opened the gift on Christmas, he exclaimed "My word! Don't let Henry see this!", referring to Henry Wallace, the Secretary of Agriculture who at the time was having young pigs slaughtered in order to control prices. The wooden pig sat on FDR's Oval Office desk throughout the rest of his administration; until the research for this book was conducted, the museum at Hyde Park had no knowledge of its origin.

It was not until 1946 that the Department of Agriculture finally issued a small Bulletin (no. 610) called *Rural Handicrafts in the United States* by Eaton and Lucinda Crile, an Extension Analyst. This document reviewed a countrywide study which had been made by Extension Services, and played an important role in the encouragement of handicrafts in the field of home economics and family life.

Crafted wooden pig from President Franklin D. Roosevelt's desk.
Courtesy of Franklin D. Roosevelt Library.

Rural Arts Exhibition, *Washington D.C., November 1937. Photo by Theodor Horydczak. Courtesy of Elizabeth and Martha Eaton.*

Rural Arts Exhibition, *Washington D.C., November 1937, miscellaneous crafts. Photo by Theodor Horydczak. Courtesy of Elizabeth and Martha Eaton.*

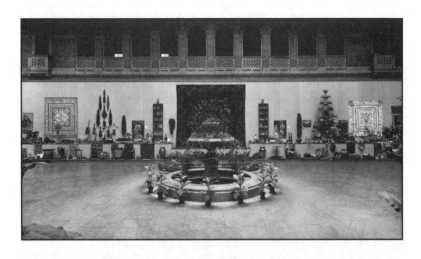

Above: Rural Arts Exhibition, *Washington D.C., November 1937. Photo by Theodor Horydczak. Courtesy of Elizabeth and Martha Eaton.*

Below: Rural Arts Exhibition, *Washington D.C., November 1937. Photo by Theodor Horydczak. Courtesy of Elizabeth and Martha Eaton.*

Rural Arts Exhibition, *Washington D.C., November 1937, basketry.*
Photo by Theodor Horydczak. Courtesy of Elizabeth and Martha Eaton.

Rural Arts Exhibition, *Washington D.C., November 1937, weaving and Indian crafts. Photo by Theodor Horydczak. Courtesy of Elizabeth and Martha Eaton.*

Rural Arts Exhibition, *Washington D.C., November 1937, miscellaneous crafts. Photo by Theodor Horydczak. Courtesy of Elizabeth and Martha Eaton.*

Rural Arts Exhibition, *Washington D.C., November 1937, handcrafted musical instruments. Photo by Theodor Horydczak. Courtesy of Elizabeth and Martha Eaton.*

Rural Arts Exhibition, *Washington D.C., November 1937, ceramics.*
Photo by Theodor Horydczak. Courtesy of Elizabeth and Martha Eaton.

Above: Rural Arts Exhibition, *Washington D.C., November 1937,* basketry. *Photo by Theodor Horydczak. Courtesy of Elizabeth and Martha Eaton.*

Below: Rural Arts Exhibition, *Washington D.C., November 1937,* children's puppets and dolls. *Photo by Theodor Horydczak. Courtesy of Elizabeth and Martha Eaton.*

In 1938, Eaton had one of the greatest honors awarded him, when he received an invitation to accept an honorary degree from the University of Oregon. The story is best told in his 1938 Christmas letter:

One day in early May, out of a clear sky and teetotally unbeknowst to me, a letter came from Donald Erb, the new President of the University of Oregon, stating that the Faculty had voted unanimously to recommend to the Board of Higher Education of Oregon that the degree of Doctor of Laws be conferred upon me, and asking if I would accept this honor.

My first reaction was that there has been a mistake somewhere, probably the girl in the office got the addresses mixed up, and maybe a notice of my delinquent alumni dues—I couldn't think of anything else they would be sending me—had been placed in the envelope and mailed to the man who would have received the notice of the doctor's degree. I figured that he would return the notice intended for me to the University and the error would be rectified. Not being in a hurry to pay my dues I just waited. But soon complications set in—congratulations came, including a wire from Mrs. Roosevelt, so I wrote the University that the rumor was getting around and if it wasn't a mistake they had better make it so, to save embarrassment to all concerned.

Well to make a long story a little bit longer, it turned out it wasn't a mistake, I mean Dr. Erb's letter, and when I had an opportunity to examine the case which four members appointed by the Faculty to investigate my record had prepared, I surrendered without a single shot. The case was a great surprise to me; they seemed to have carefully brought together everything I had done since, as a very young man, I innocently leaped into fame as an enemy of society for telling the people of Eugene during the great typhoid epidemic to boil their drinking water, to the time when, during the World War, I turned Traitor to my country by insisting that those with whom I differed should be protected in their rights of assembly and of free speech. But more gratifying than anything else was a careful documentation of the work I have done since leaving my native state about twenty years ago. While it was weighted on the side of what I have tried to do—rather than what I have accomplished—yet I must say it was a fine, dignified impressive statement, quite the greatest tribute I have ever received, and I shall strive always to deserve it. The citation read on the commencement program as follows:

HONORARY DEGREE
Doctor of Laws
Conferred upon
Allen Hendershott Eaton

In recognition of his foresight and courage as legislator, citizen, and public servant; his tireless endeavor in promoting an appreciation of beauty in art and creative craftsmanship, and his sympathetic and enlightened understanding of the vital contributions which foreign peoples have made to the culture and civilization of America.

I wish that I had some way of letting those who were responsible for this honor know my true feelings about it; but I think they do. If anything could bring me closer to the University to which I owe a debt that I can never repay (I am not referring to my alumni dues) it is this unanimous action by men and women whom I so thoroughly respect . . .

I must turn now to another satisfaction which the year just closing has brought to me. I refer to a new buck-saw which I came across down in Patterson's Hardware Store in Park Row in June. About the time I discovered this saw I remembered that I was having a doctor's degree conferred on me in absentia out in Lane County, Oregon, which once had more standing timber than any county in the United States, and partly because of this connection I decided to make myself a commencement present of a buck-saw; and oh boy it has proved a lollapullilah. I might say in passing that about the only thing the Faculty overlooked in bringing my achievements together was my record in wood cutting. I did mean to have, for this letter, my picture taken with my doctor's hood, my wood cutting tools, including the new buck-saw, my sledge, and my three old wedges, Shem, Ham and Jaspeth, but we couldn't get around to it.

Since this letter goes to some rather illiterate people who do not know of such things, I should say something about my doctor's hood, a stunning piece of wearing apparel which came out of a clear sky too. It has wide purple facing, I think you would call it, very royal in appearance which hangs down the front like a bib; and the lining of lemon yellow and green (The University of Oregon's colors) which hangs down the back is beautiful. I don't know why it is called a hood, though it would serve that purpose in case of rain. The evening I brought it home we spent in trying it on in different ways. I will not go into that now, but all the family was interested. It is without doubt the most impressive garment—if I may call it that—which has ever been in our family, excepting possibly Cecile's wedding dress and the evening suit Mrs. Davis made for me when I was a member of the Oregon Glee Club . . .the costume was very effective

*from a considerable distance but it had little of the
intrinsic quality of this hood. The hood looks best I
think when worn over something dark. That night
before retiring I tried it over my B.V.D's thinking
that there might be some affinity between the letters
L.L.D. and B.V.D., but there really isn't much.*

⸎

The progress of writing *Handicrafts of the Southern Highlands* moved along steadily during these years. As early as
1933 Eaton had found a photographer to use for the illustrations which would accompany the text, and this was Doris
Ulmann. Mrs. Ulmann was well-known and had spent some
time in the Southern Highlands doing work, so her interests
directly related to Eaton's. From 1933 until her death in 1934,
she traveled extensively with Clem recording craftspeople and
other subjects which Clem felt would fit into Eaton's idea of
what illustrative material was needed. Upon Doris Ulmann's
death there were over 2,000 plates from which Eaton could
select for his book. A Doris Ulmann Foundation had been
established, and Eaton was appointed to the Ulmann Foundation to help distribute the photographs to carry out Mrs.
Ulmann's interest that they be used to bring together the arts
and social work. There was much correspondence between
Eaton and the Russell Sage Foundation concerning Ulmann's
gift of the use of the photographs. After issues of money and
of the number of photographs that could be used were settled,
the problem of the illustrations was resolved. The original photographic plates now rest in the Doris Ulmann Foundation in
Berea, Kentucky, although originally the Ulmann Foundation
operated out of the offices of the Russell Sage Foundation.

Once *Handicrafts of the Southern Highlands* was published, it received glowing reviews from all directions, but
most importantly it encouraged Eaton to write many articles
on the indigenous handicrafts of America. The book established him as the high lord of American crafts, placing him in

the position of being invited to give even more lectures and to direct handicraft exhibitions.

The book caught the personality and character of the mountain people. His writing illustrated his love for the region and the romanticism of the Southern Highlands. The craftpeople loved it. The book sold well, and of course finally went out of print, as most books do. However, in 1973, it was republished by Dover Press, after the rights had been sold to them without any royalties going to the family.

The only difference between the reissue and the Russell Sage Foundation publication is the introduction in the Dover Press edition written by Rayna Green. In the first part she speaks highly of Eaton and his ability to report on the technology of the crafts, but later questions his romanticizing of the Highlands and their crafts and lifestyle. She especially also questions his research techniques in the field, not really understanding the significance of his initial leadership in looking at handicrafts and social problems together. She misquotes his definition of art out of context, which makes Eaton appear to be a writer unsure of his aesthetic judgment.

In Eaton's 1941 Christmas letter he repeats his definition of art: "Art is not the thing that is done, but the way in which it is done; an object of art may be a painting on canvas, a sculpture in bronze, or a cathedral in stone, but it may also be a woodpile or a haystack." Rayna Green did not understand what Eaton was about when she wrote her educational-jargon-filled introduction in 1973 about the 1930s.

Another quote of Eaton's that is very important to his work throughout his life involves the word *handicrafts*. When the Guild was formed it chose Southern Highlands Handicraft Guild for its name. There were many times during the ensuing years when various persons wished to change the name, but as long as Eaton was alive, there was a group of people within the Guild who refused to see this happen. Eaton was very convinced that the word handicraft was preferable to crafts or any other word which might be chosen. He used the term handicrafts throughout his life, even after the word craft had become a household word in the field of making objects in an artistic and creative manner. Eaton defines the word, which bears repeating, in the preface of the *Southern Highlands* book:

> *The word 'handicraft,' as used in this report, is a broad term including all those things which people make with their hands either for their own use or for that of others. The article may be fashioned entirely by hand, including the preparation of all material even to the shaping of the tools employed, or it may be made in part by machinery as in the preparation of woods for fine cabinet work, or as in the machine spinning of thread and yarn to be woven on the hand loom; but if the final product, the character of the thing itself, is shaped by hand, it is an object of handicraft.*

As the decade of the 1930s drew to an end, Eaton was looking onward to other adventures in his pursuit of working with the handicrafts. He had many projects which had been shelved away while he developed his work in exhibitions and in the Southern Highlands.

During the writing and collecting of material for *Handicrafts of the Southern Highlands*, he kept his connections with the American Federation of Art and the Art Alliance of America. He also served on committees of the Council on Adult Education for the Foreign-Born, the Foreign Language Information Service, and the American Institute of Graphic Arts, of which he was at one time the director and a vice president. He was involved with the Tennessee Valley Authority in an attempt to bring about the merging of various small craft programs. Eventually these Southern Highland groups joined with the Guild.

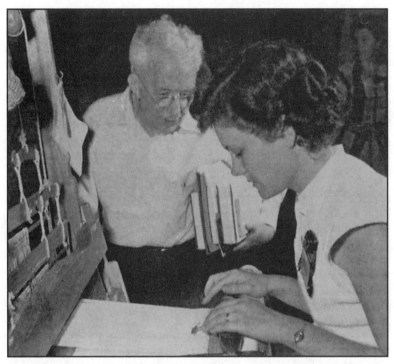

Mary Sandler, Berea College student, demonstrates weaving to Eaton at Summer Workshop, 1950. Courtesy of Arrowmont School of Arts and Crafts.

Summer workshop staff of Pi Beta Phi School, 1950. (Left to right) Allen Eaton, Mary Elizabeth Starr Sullivan, Helen Watson, Barbara McDonald, Jane Glass, Ruth Dyer, Marian Heard, Berta Frey, Marguerite Horn. Courtesy of Arrowmont School of Arts and Crafts.

Handicrafts Of New England

To believe that everyone in our democracy counts and to encourage each to make his best contributions is to give special significance to handicrafts because here is by far the largest field of artistic expression in the visual arts, and here countless persons throughout America, hitherto unknown, are making modest, skillful, original, and often beautiful things which reflect their mental world and the elements of their environment.

Allen Eaton, *Handicrafts of New England*

Ceramics by Edwin and Mary Scheier of Durham, New Hampshire. Photo by Edmund de Beaumond from Handicrafts of New England.

105

Allen Eaton's interest in the handicrafts of New England came early in his work with the Russell Sage Foundation. He was not unfamiliar with New England; he loved to brag that his family had originated from there before they migrated to Oregon, and in several of his Christmas letters he devoted a goodly amount of space to his New England heritage. Professionally he had visited many different areas in New England, which had given him a strong impression of the handicrafts in that region. In 1943, he gave an address at the University of Maine in Orono to extension workers, and he also had traveled in the late 1930s and early 1940s to Connecticut, New Hampshire, and various other New England destinations to speak on handicrafts.

According to the Russell Sage Foundation archives, Eaton had requests in 1928 to make a survey of New England handicrafts, but because of his other duties at the Foundation, he was unable to follow through. By 1929, Eaton had suggested a variety of studies which could be conducted by his department. Among these were *The Arts and Crafts in American Homes*, *The Influence of Beauty in the Lives of Working People*, and *The Arts and Crafts in Boys' and Girls' Clubs*. In January 1942, in a memo to Shelby Harrison, he listed part of the work program of the Department of Arts and Social Work, a *Study of Handicrafts in the New England States*.

Eaton had been appointed as an adviser to the New Hampshire Commission of Arts and Crafts in 1931. New Hampshire was the first state in the country to form such an organization, and it was this commission which eventually created the League of New Hampshire Arts and Crafts in 1932. Eaton was active in the organization but his work with the Southern Highlands project always came first. He did attend nine of the League's summer craft fairs, and was very involved in getting them ready each year. His influence in the commission is very evident, for one of its prime responsibilities was working with surveys.

The first Fair of the League of New Hampshire Arts and Crafts was held in 1934 at Crawford Notch, four years after

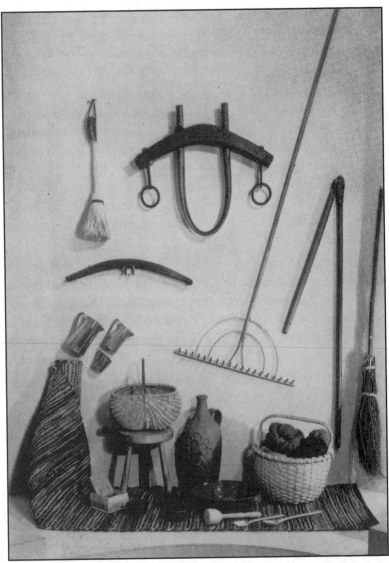

A *selection of handicrafts from the* Farm And Home in New England States Exhibition. *Photo by Edmund de Beaumont. Photo from* Handicrafts of New England.

Belle D. Robinson, a maker of braided rugs in New England. Photo by Doris Day. Photo from Handicrafts of New England.

the first Southern Highlanders (not to be confused with the Southern Highland Handicraft Guild) held theirs in 1930, in Knoxville, Tennessee. The League was well organized, Mrs. Jacob Randolph Coolidge as its first president. Mrs. Coolidge was active in the 1937 *Rural Art Exhibition* in Washington, providing handicrafts from New England and working along with Eaton and Clementine Douglas in the preparation of the exhibition. Throughout the growth of the League and the Southern Highland Handicraft Guild, there was a close exchange among them of letters and information to help in bringing about good markets, educational programs, and a better understanding of American handicrafts by the public. The League became an important element in the craft world, and eventually from its ranks came David B. Campbell, who was to play such a strong role in the American Crafts Council after Mrs. Aileen Vanderbilt Webb established it in 1940.

The New Hampshire League and the Southern Highland Handicraft Guild were basically attempting to do the same things, and that was, and still is, to help regional craftsmen find better markets for their handicrafts, to enrich family life through various educational programs in the arts, and to give a sense of direction to the work of rural people in those particular areas. Eaton's aims and goals were the same, except that he also wanted to record the traditional handicrafts, and bring about a better understanding of these people to their fellow citizens of the United States, much as he had done with the immigrants in the early 1920s. His philosophic goals were deeply entrenched in the concept of merging the arts with social work.

The fieldwork for gathering information on the craftsmen in New England was especially difficult, because most of the work was done after gas rationing had gone into effect, leaving transportation mainly to trains which did not reach the isolated areas. In a long and detailed report to Shelby Harrison on June 24, 1944, Eaton pointed out " . . .in the spring we shall hope to get enough gasoline somehow to reach the more remote places which must be visited." It is difficult to determine how much of

New Hampshire folk whittler Archie Gilbert. Photo by Doris Day from Handicrafts of New England.

the field work he was doing himself, and how much was being carried out by other staff members for in his reports he alternately uses the terms "I" and "we." Whether the "we" is editorial or plural is unknown; it may refer to his daughter Martha Eaton, who did the driving for him, since Eaton did not drive himself.

An event which helped Eaton greatly in collecting material for his project was the *Exhibition of Contemporary New England Handicrafts* held at the Worcester Art Museum in Worcester, Massachusetts. On July 30, 1942, the director, Charles H. Sawyer, gathered a group of people to examine the possibilities of having an exhibition of New England crafts. Eaton was not only a part of this group, but he was also the major collector of the handicrafts which were to be shown. For over a year, Eaton amassed many objects which would reflect the work of rural handicrafters in the New England region.

The exhibition opened on October 14, 1943, and ran until December 26, 1943, with hundreds of handicrafts. Featured were beautifully handwoven yard goods and typically New England crafted weather vanes and hand carved birds. In one part of the exhibit, in a small museum installation called *Cottage Alcove*, there was a corner of a New England room which illustrated the handicrafts of the region as they might appear in an average home. Wallpaper, draperies, furniture, and other objects all gave the museum visitor a view of how handicrafts could be utilized in everyday life.

While every craftsman imaginable was represented from the Northeast, the work of Edwin and Mary Scheier seemed to be very prominent in this exhibition. Both of the Scheiers were to become nationally known for their pioneer work in ceramics as the late 20th century craft renaissance progressed.

Several photographers were used to record the exhibition, but the two most important were Doris Day, a Connecticut photographer, and Edmund de Beaumont, of Worcester, Massachusetts. Eaton had acquired the services of Day through the

Foundation, while de Beaumont was retained by the Worcester Art Museum. From the work of these photographers Eaton obtained most of his photographs for his New England book.

Eaton was not only involved in the actual collection of the objects, but was also very influential in the production of the exhibition catalog. The catalog's visual appearance illustrates Eaton's strong influence on its design. As in most of Eaton's books, the last page is dedicated to giving credits to the typographical characteristics of the layout. He was very fond of Caledonia typeface designed by William Addison Dwiggins, a designer and craftsman from Hingham, Massachusetts, and used it not only for the New England book, but also both *Beauty Behind Barbed Wire* and *Beauty for the Sighted and the Blind*.

In the Introduction for the catalog, titled *The New England Exhibition and the American Handicrafts Movement*, Eaton wrote a brief history of the Arts and Crafts Movement that had originated in England and how it had continued in New England. He gives credit to the Society of Arts and Crafts of Boston as playing a fundamental role in establishing handicraft societies throughout New England, and also points out that New Hampshire was the first state in the country to establish a Commission for Arts and Crafts, which Governor Winant appointed in 1931. This commission could be considered the official beginning of the crafts movement in New England as it existed in 1943. With Eaton as part of the Commission, and with his part in the Worcester exhibition, there is little question that his input was of significant importance in the development of handicrafts in New England.

In the Introduction, Eaton lists five important values in relation to handicrafts:

> There are at least five great values that come to workers through the practice of handicrafts: the economics, the social, the educational, the therapeutic, and the esthetic. And any one may be

quite as important to the craftsman as another. But it should always be remembered that the appreciation of any one of these values does not exclude another.

By social value is meant the sense of satisfaction which comes from doing something that another appreciates, and also the pleasure that often comes from doing work together.

The educational value of handicrafts is illustrated in two ways, both based on learning by doing. The late President Eliot of Harvard said, 'Accurate work with carpenter's tools, or lathe or hammer and anvil, or violin or piano, or pencil or crayon, or camel's hair brush, trains well the same nerves and ganglia with which we do what is ordinarily called thinking.' There is in the practice of any handicraft a basis of interest for research and learning which makes it one of the most promising of subjects for adult education. The basic principle in adult education is to start with an established interest. I know three new England men who wove cloth for their own suits on hand looms: each one says that he learned more about cloth, and the history of textiles through this experience than he had learned in all his life before.

The therapeutic value of work with the hands is in all our minds today, as it never had been before, because of the soldiers, sailors and fliers in our armed forces whose recovery from wounds and shock will depend upon this correlation of hand and mind. . . .The curative value of hand work for maimed bodies and sick minds is too well known to need argument here; but it would be well if more of us realized the exercises that will cure also prevent.

The esthetic satisfactions which come through handicrafts must ever be counted among their greatest values. The practice of any handicrafts gives an opportunity for the creation and enjoyment of beauty, one of the greatest human privileges, and to many, an indispensable experience in the pursuit of happiness.

Courtesy of Worcester Museum of Art

Eaton was quick to establish that there was a uniqueness about the New England handicrafts, just as there was a special character about those objects made in the Southern Highlands. The qualities of each were determined by cultural differences, geographic differences, and ethnic differences. This was important for Eaton in his search for the unique identities of people of all kinds living in this melting pot country. Model ship building reflected the occupations of seafarers in New England, while the dulcimer was a part of the musical traditions in the mountains of the Southern Highlands.

When Eaton finished his work on the book about the Southern Highlands, he had many other projects in the works. One of these, which spanned several years, was a film *America's Making*, dealing with the problems of ethnic groups, immigrants, and the concept of national unity. He was very excited about working on this film, which was not a part of his work at the Foundation, but which did include several people from the Foundation on the Sponsoring Committee. He had many problems with obtaining money for this project, but eventually, he involved Eleanor Roosevelt in its promotion and funding.

Eaton had long been corresponding with Mrs. Roosevelt. Ever since his involvement with her during the *Rural Arts Exhibition* in 1937, he had kept up a fairly regular letter writing campaign in order to keep her informed on the status of handicrafts. On August 30, 1937, he sent her a copy of *Handicrafts of the Southern Highlands*. "I am sending you herewith the first copy of *Handicrafts of the Southern Highlands* to come from the bindery, and in due time you will receive a bill as requested. I appreciate, as do other members of the Foundation, the interest you have expressed in this report . . .I am giving myself the pleasure of sending you one of my 'author's copies' bound for you in linen woven in the Highlands. Please do not acknowledge it; you are doing too many worthwhile things to do so."

However, Mrs. Roosevelt answered on September 7, 1937, "I am delighted with the book you sent and am especially pleased to have the linen binding. I would not think of failing to thank you for your thought of me."

The next year she wrote to him when she heard that he was to receive the honorary degree from the University of Oregon, and in future years referred to him questions that she had received about handicrafts.

On June 20, 1940, Eaton wrote to Mrs. Roosevelt that selections from *America's Making* would be shown on June 5, 1940, but that if she couldn't make that screening, he could make the film available at another time. After several letters between Eaton and Mrs. Roosevelt, it was agreed that she would see the film at the Preview Theatre in New York on July 8 after she had attended a luncheon the same day at La Guardia Field. She was interested enough in the film to instruct the Friends Service Committee to send Eaton $500.00.

The letters continued to be exchanged for several years, often with Eaton ending with a note that she give FDR his regards.

On November 4, 1940, Eaton sent her a handwritten note: "Tomorrow my family. Four of us (I wish we were four thousand), will cast four votes for the President who has done more for our country and our world than any other in our time. Whatever the outcome, I want to record here, as at the polls, our deep gratitude for what he is and has done; and we pray that he may have many, many strong and happy years ahead . . .And every wish for him is a wish for you to whom our admiration and affection go out in fullest measure, for you have made, as Wife of the President, of our dear United States, a great new and secure place in the minds, the hearts, and lives of countless citizens. To them you have been—and ever will be—the finest democrat of us all. Faithfully yours, Allen Eaton and Family."

Music box made by Martha Eaton for Eleanor Roosevelt at Val-Kill cottage. Courtesy of Franklin D. Roosevelt Library.

The letter has an attachment "RETURN TO MRS. ROOS-EVELT—The President has seen" (*sic*). Eleanor Roosevelt thanked Eaton for his heartening and loyal confidence in the administration.

The final status of the film *America's Making* is not known, although several preliminary reviews were made by various people during its filming. It is likely that it was never completed nor shown nationally, as Eaton had envisioned.

During the 1940s, Eaton and his Department of Arts and Social Work provided many other services throughout the United States. In 1940 alone the Foundation lists the following activities for that year:

> . . . they included the following range, which may be regarded as fairly typical: advice on an international exhibition of handicrafts, on a handicrafts exhibit at the Museum of Modern Art, and on murals for the American Common at the New York World's Fair; information furnished to a director of handicraft work in Kentucky, to a teacher of weaving considering employment with the Farm Security Administration, to a director of arts and crafts in a settlement in Pittsburgh, to the United States Department of Agriculture on a handicraft program for the extension division; consultation with writers on material on the Southern Highlands, on folklore, on the League of New Hampshire Arts and Crafts, on handicrafts at Arthurdale, West Virginia, on publication of explorations in Mexico, on a unit of Visualized Curriculum Series on contributions to America of the foreign born; aid to workers in the field with respect to photographing rural scenes, weaving, metalworking, co-operative workshops for the National Youth Administration, activities of the Lutheran Mission in North Carolina, activities of the

Farm Security Administration, consultations with a
representative of the All Indian National Congress
and with students of handicrafts in Scandinavia.

By the mid-forties, Eaton was well aware that his retirement was imminent, and he was very concerned that he would
not be able to complete his work at the Foundation. He had
appealed often to the Trustees to let him continue his work,
and made his strongest plea in 1943, the year for his retirement,
with a 14-page memo covering the list of those projects yet to
be completed. In this list was *The Study of the Handicrafts of
New England, An Exhibit of Objects of Beauty for the Blind*,
Schaefer-Simmern's project, *Articles on Rural Arts and the
Department of Agriculture Bulletin*, and a *Report on the Origin
and History of the Department of Arts and Social Work*.

Eaton was able to postpone his retirement for three years,
but in October 1946, he finally was defeated and left the Foundation. This left many of his dreams still unfulfilled. Eaton's
manuscript for *Handicrafts of New England* was substantially
complete, and the Foundation saw it as a significant addition to
the knowledge of handicrafts and arts, which they had already
sponsored. However, by the time of the book's completion, the
Foundation had changed its mind and the book was published
by another press; the exact reason for not continuing this project cannot be found in the Foundation archives.

Eaton writes in his 1947 Christmas letter about his disappointment concerning the status of his department after he
left.

*I have had one grievance, a very great one, that the
Department of Arts and Social Work which has struck
new notes in the social field and could contribute so
much to the world situation, is not to be continued.
I gave the best I had in laying a basis upon which a
good structure of service could be built, and we were
considering an unusual man who could have carried*

the work to higher levels, but the Foundation's finances had undergone a great strain and I could not make a case in the face of serious budget situations. So when the decision to discontinue the Department was made I could do nothing but acquiesce with sorrow that the institution which has become dear to me should lose one of its fine and vital opportunities and that the idea which I thought had attained continuity had come to failure. My work was based upon the simple concept that beauty is one of the great human forces which those dealing with social problems should know about and should find ways of using through a wider and deeper appreciation of the arts and man. Something of what we have accomplished in this comparatively new department is recorded in the History of the Foundation, *recently published: but is little compared to much that is waiting close at hand to be done. I should couple with this expression of disappointment that gratitude I feel to the Foundation for what we were permitted to do together and for making possible some of the publications and projects the influence of which I hope and believe will extend into the future.*

Once the Foundation had declined to publish the New England book, Eaton was on his own to find a publisher. In his Christmas letters he speaks about the problems of being rejected several times, mainly because various publishing houses felt the book was of regional interest only and would not justify printing. There was a concern that only 4,000 copies could be sold, and the price of printing such a book would mean higher cost and even less sales. But finally, Eaton writes in his 1949 Christmas letter:

First barrel. The year 1948, reported upon just twelve months ago, had been to the wood chopper and his family the nearest approach to one of tribulation

*since they left their native Oregon more than 30 years
ago to become permanent citizens of New York State.
A suggestion of the nature and extent of the situation
then was indicated by the following entry in his diary
in early December 1948, which read 'Spirits none
too high today'. After long and trying delay, Boston
publisher has turned down* Handicrafts of New
England *manuscript . . .Just to give variety to life
my neighbor has sued me and the old beech tree out
our kitchen door, for $5,000, trespass damages, and
costs, and demands that the tree, which he says is a
continuous menace, be cut down.*

*Second barrel. An entry in my diary in the
spring reads: 'This day, April the 14th in the year
of Our Lord 1949; the 173rd year of our country's
independence; and 20th of our life in Crestwood will
long be remembered with praise and thanksgiving
by the Eaton family because on this day Harper and
Brothers signed a contract to publish* Handicrafts of
New England; *and the Supreme Court of Westchester
County at White Plains decided that there was no
trespass; there was not damage, and the old beech
tree should stand.*

Being an old woodchopper, Eaton had mentioned this tree in
previous letters to his family and friends, but he recapped the
story in the 1949 letter to insure that everyone understand his
glee at winning the suit.

*. . .as to the old beech tree; while our neighbor has
for years threatened to cut off the limbs extending
over the property line, we have in each case done
something to prevent it, succeeding mainly because
cutting could not be done without climbing the tree,
which, of course, is on our lot, and we controlled the
climbing. During these controversial years we have
cut many limbs at his request, and others which*

I thought justified, until there seemed to me no reasonable grounds fur (sic) cutting more. But our neighbor was not satisfied and in October brought suit to compel me to remove the tree and pay him $5,000 for root and limb trespass damages. I should give you the fight round by round, but this is not the time and place for it. However, as in the fight for the book, we lost most of the battles but the last one, and the beech stands as a monument to the family who fought, bled and mighty nigh died for the love of a grand old tree.

In this letter he also reports that he is again writing on the arts of the Japanese-Americans in relocation camps, and on the research for his book which he had tentatively titled *Objects of Beauty for the Blind.*

Eaton was very involved with writing, knowing that his income was meager, and that he needed to keep at least a small amount of money coming into the household. Both his *Immigrant* and the *Southern Highlands* books were published by the Foundation as reports of his work within the context of his position. Only his *New England* book would bring in royalties, and like most art books, probably not in any great amount.

But I must hang up on the book and say a word about the tree, for if I had to choose between borning a book and saving a tree, I—well—isn't it wonderful to be able to do both in one year—and, as I have recorded, to have them come on the same day. In a hundred years from now I will look down upon 1949—or will I be looking up—as one of the best years of a full and wonderful life on earth. And to all the little cherubs gathered around me, or to the little imps—and it will probably be a mixture of both—I will tell much more about the beech tree and other things I can write down here. I estimate that our beech tree is a little more than two hundred years old, based upon another in the same forest a mile away, undermined by excavating for gravel, that blew over a few years ago, and which I cut up. It was a sapling in 1776. The crown of our tree is still the finest of 50 beeches within a three mile radius of our cottage, and how we enjoy it since it was saved. I missed its companionship for six weeks this summer while I was in Gatlinburg, but there were compensations in two fine beeches on the side of the hill not far from the workshop. I will never forget one evening when we saw them, and their wonderful roots in the last rays of the setting sun. Once again I saw them very early in the morning when I went out to see sunflowers in a nearby field, and to pick a tiny one for a new friend going on a journey, with its wonderful miniature spiral seed pattern—as perfect as in a larger flower. I got back to Crestwood well in time to hear the 'seed fall' from our beech in September; which is one of the lovely sounds at the end of the summer. I will try to describe a beech 'seed fall' sometime; it usually goes on for three days and three nights. It is next to the gentlest sound I have ever heard in our little yard—the gentlest being the flight of a barn owl that once came down our chimney and flew from our back porch into the night.

Beauty Behind Barbed Wire

. . .we have taken stock of our stake in America and now we are preparing in a new spirit to reestablish ourselves.

Manzanar Free Press, *January 1, 1944.*

One of Mr. Tsunekawa's dwarf daisy chrysanthemums at Rohwer, Arkansas Relocation Center. Photo by Paul Faris from Beauty Behind Barbed Wire. *Copyright © 1952 by Allen H. Eaton. Copyright © renewed 1980 by Martha Eaton and Elizabeth Eaton. Reprinted by permission of HarperCollins Publishers Inc.*

In 1942, Eaton, along with many thousands of other citizens of the United States, was shocked to hear that Japanese-Americans were to be relocated from their homes in the western states of California, Oregon and Washington, to internment camps away from the coastal region. This move was instigated by Franklin Delano Roosevelt's Presidential Executive Order No. 9066 on the 19th of February 1942, and it was claimed that such an act was necessary for the national security. 110,000 *Issei* (1st generation) and *Nissei* (2nd generation) were relocated and sent to ten camps in the interior of the United States. Of these internees, 70,000 were born in America and were citizens, while the rest were ineligible for citizenship in those days.

This incredible action took away the civil liberties of people who were citizens of this country, merely because it was possible to identify them racially, an extreme case of what we would now call racial profiling. The same relocation was not deemed necessary by the War Relocation Authority (WRA) for citizens of Italian and German ancestry. The Japanese-Americans not only lost their homes to property scavengers and quick money-makers, but they also lost all their personal possessions, bank accounts, and most important, their rights to be participating American citizens in a country in which most of them had been born.

Immediately after World War II was over, many books appeared on the scene describing the events and problems surrounding the removal of these disenfranchised people. One of these books, *Beauty Behind Barbed Wire: The Arts of the Japanese in our War Relocation Camps* by Allen Eaton was published in 1952 by Harper & Brothers with a foreword by his friend Eleanor Roosevelt. The book itself is 208 pages, but of those pages only a small number deal with the account of the Japanese relocation process and problems. Most of the book concerns itself with the various methods used by the Japanese-American internees to enrich their lives during the stay in the camps.

Above: A Relocation Center camp in the desert. Photo by Francis Stewart. Below: A Relocation Center art fair. Courtesy of Elizabeth and Martha Eaton. Photos from Beauty Behind Barbed Wire. Copyright © 1952 by Allen H. Eaton. *Copyright © renewed 1980 by Martha Eaton and Elizabeth Eaton. Reprinted by permission of HarperCollins Publishers Inc.*

Drawing by Mine Okubo from Citizen 13660 *showing Japanese-Americans being sent to a War Relocation Center. Courtesy of Mine Okubo.*

Early in 1942, when Eaton heard of the program he immediately started to work on plans to conduct exhibitions of handicrafts in the War Relocation Centers. His main intent in a project of this nature was that

> *. . .an exhibition would suggest that our nation is made up of people from many homelands and that there still were many Americans aware of this, who appreciated the rich and varied contributions our immigrant people have brought to our life and culture. Such an exhibition, I felt, would help overcome the barriers of language; it might give these internees a sense of their relatedness to many friendly people outside; another important thing—it might encourage some of them to make things with their own hands—this would help ease mental strains, and possibly contribute to a good community spirit.*

The Japanese, more than any people I knew had a genius for making something out of almost nothing, so scarcity of materials need not be considered a deterrent.

(*Beauty Behind Barbed Wire*, p.3)

This concept was not unlike his work with immigrant handicrafts. However, in the exhibitions he planned for this project there would be handicrafts of the various ethnic groups in the United States, and they would be taken to the Japanese-Americans in the relocation centers. While some of the objects might be created by Japanese-Americans, a great percentage would be from other immigrant people in our country.

Eaton approached Dill Meyer, the director of the War Relocation Authority, for help in assembling an exhibition of various handicrafts to send on tour to the internment camps, but was refused. Meyer felt that it would appear that the government was coddling the internees, and he further asserted that funds were just not available for such a project, especially since money was being allocated for photographic essays on activities in the camps.

Eaton wanted not only to bring beauty and light into the lives of the people in the centers, but he also wanted to encourage them to create for themselves. Meyer, who was not opposed to the idea, encouraged him to have the Russell Sage Foundation support such a project, but the Foundation felt it . . . "was not then in a position to help." This comment makes one wonder whether the Foundation may have been a little fearful to participate in an activity which seemed to favor the Japanese-Americans, especially at a time when "coddling Japs" would not improve one's reputation, and would be looked upon with disfavor and suspicion throughout the United States. Especially in the western states, any Oriental was suspect of being an enemy, and anyone showing partiality would certainly bring discomfort upon his head. There is no proof that this was why Eaton was refused by the Foundation, but the manner in

Bobby Kaneko dressed as a flower for the play Mary, Mary, Quite Contrary. *Photo by Francis Stewart. Photo from* Beauty Behind Barbed Wire. Copyright © 1952 by Allen H. Eaton. *Copyright © renewed 1980 by Martha Eaton and Elizabeth Eaton. Reprinted by permission of HarperCollins Publishers Inc.*

which he states the refusal leaves the question in the mind of the readers. The only other reason would be the feeling of the Foundation that Eaton was getting close to retirement and that a new project would not be completed in time, since Eaton was slow, meticulous and thorough in all his work.

With the refusal of the Foundation and the WRA, and the fact that Eaton had many other obligations with the Foundation, it was necessary that he temporarily give up the idea of preparing handicraft exhibitions for the relocation centers. As the idea fermented, he worked on his New England project. However, he was still very sure that an exhibition would not only enrich the lives of the interned, but that an exhibition which included the creative work of the Japanese-American community would help bring about a better understanding of their characteristics to the American public.

It was not long after the Foundation's refusal, but apparently still in 1942, that Eaton received through the mails some small and beautifully polished stones which had been carefully worked by one of the internees, and in the next few months, he continued to receive various gifts made by different people in the camps. He realized that even without his encouragement, the internees were fast at work creating with materials they could find. More than ever, he was determined that an exhibition should take place, but not necessarily of other American immigrant work, but of that of the Japanese-Americans.

Eaton's book, as the dust jacket maintains, " . . .is a story without parallel in this country." Mrs. Roosevelt's foreword is a glowing approval of his book, and at the same time an admiring endorsement of the WRA. It is rather surprising that Mrs. Roosevelt's foreword does not in any way mention the injustices of relocation centers, nor the civil rights which were so blatantly taken away from the Japanese-Americans. She, in fact, commends the work of the WRA in relation to the centers and evacuees. Her foreword is superficial, and gives little indication of the humanitarianism which she so vigorously displayed later in her work with the United Nations. In the fifteen or twenty

A miniature Japanese garden at Poston, Arizona Relocation Center. Photo by Francis Stewart from Beauty Behind Barbed Wire. *Copyright © 1952 by Allen H. Eaton. Copyright © renewed 1980 by Martha Eaton and Elizabeth Eaton. Reprinted by permission of HarperCollins Publishers*

pages of the text not devoted to art or crafts concerns, Eaton does mention some of the unpleasant aspects of the centers; but in general his book is a flowery treatise on the beauty of the handicrafts of the Japanese-Americans. Eaton was not a confrontational person and most of his work seldom illustrated any negative aspects.

It was only after Eaton realized the unlikelihood of securing funding that he decided to take some vacation time in the summer of 1945 in order to visit the relocation camps himself to record what was taking place there. While he visited five of the camps, he had photographers and assistants visit the other four camps. By this time, Camp Jerome, in Arkansas, had been closed down.

Of the many books which have appeared on the internment of the Japanese-Americans, none of them cover in detail the artistic accomplishments of these people during their years of imprisonment. Allen R. Bosworth, author of *America's Concentrations Camps*, does mention Eaton's book in his bibliography, and the personal observations of Mime Okubo in her book *Citizen 13660* briefly mention the creative endeavors of the interns; but most of the published material investigates the government administration, legal concerns, military action and the logistical aspects of the Japanese-American relocation.

Mime Okubo wrote on June 2, 1975, "I first met Mr. Eaton in 1946 at my exhibition of 'Japanese evacuation and camp life' ... here in New York and at that time he showed great interest in the Japanese Evacuation. It was not long after that he contacted me requesting names to see in the camps as he worked to do a book on crafts and hobby in the camps. Later I heard that he had visited the camps and in 1952 I received a copy of his book . . .He was short and dignified—a man with snow-white hair but alive with awareness and interest. A very alert and easy person to converse with, shy but aggressive and with a drive."

Other authors mentioned only in passing the handicrafts which were taking place during the evacuees' internment,

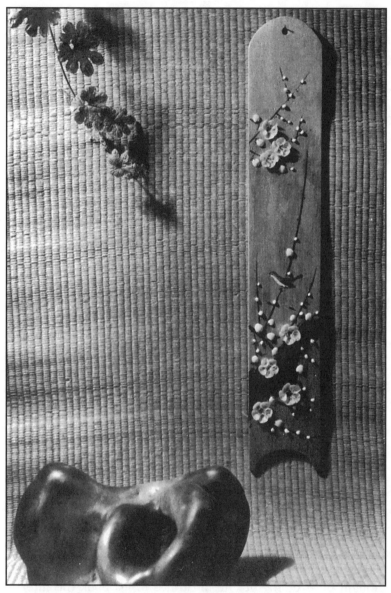

A group of objects made by Japanese-Americans in Relocation Center. A kobu is in the foreground. Photo by Toyo Miyatake from Beauty Behind Barbed Wire. Copyright © 1952 by Allen H. Eaton. *Copyright © renewed 1980 by Martha Eaton and Elizabeth Eaton. Reprinted by permission of HarperCollins Publishers Inc.*

but Eaton found many people working in the arts in order to enrich their personal lives. One aspect which other authors also mentioned was the interest of the internees in beautifying the landscape surrounding the barracks in the compounds. In the midst of the deserts, they managed to create lovely Japanese gardens, planted victory gardens of vegetables and fruit, and dug small ponds and lakes by which they could meditate and think out their problems.

Eaton looked very romantically on the handicrafts and lives of the Japanese-Americans, much as he had in his books about the Southern Highlands and New England craftsmen. In this respect Rayna Green, in her introduction to the Dover Press edition of the Southern Highlands book, was correct. His book dwells primarily on the beauty which resulted from the efforts of a few people, and little on the many troubles that beset them in their daily tasks of eating, sleeping, and generally living in desperate conditions. There were unquestionably many unhappy experiences in the centers which must have colored the lives of the internees. In fact, Alexander H. Leighton's book *The Governing of Men* places a great deal of stress on the strike to protest conditions which took place at the Poston camp located near Parker, Arizona.

However, *Beauty Behind Barbed Wire* is a simpler and more direct book, which brings a deep understanding to the reader of the character of the Japanese-Americans—their relationship to their past cultural heritage and their profound commitment to the American culture in which they lived.

Eaton, as usual, saw more than just the handicrafts that the people made, for he was also intensely interested in their way of life. He includes not only those objects which are today thought of as crafts, but he illustrates in his book the interiors of the barracks and how families attempted to make their environment an acceptable place in which to live. He spends a great deal of time showing the art of *bon-kei* (miniature landscape) and the accomplishments of outdoor landscaping.

A skilled master of calligraphy at the Rohwer, Arkansas Relocation Center. Photo by Paul Faris from Beauty Behind Barbed Wire. Copyright © 1952 by Allen H. Eaton. *Copyright © renewed 1980 by Martha Eaton and Elizabeth Eaton. Reprinted by permission of HarperCollins Publishers Inc.*

One important part of the women's lives was the study and pursuit of *ikebana* (flower arrangement). In *ikebana*, the use of native and indigenous American plants can be seen in contrast to the formal techniques of creating beautiful arrangements, which were traditionally used along with ornamental writing and symbolic drawings for *tokonoma*, or raised alcoves in the home.

Wood carving was one of the handicrafts which was very popular in the centers, and Eaton was interested in the varied approaches to this craft. Because wood was available in most locations, and because it was inexpensive, the men especially found great joy in working with it. Many people made and collected *kobus*, beautifully finished pieces of wood found in their natural state and polished by hand. Generally a tree root or part of a trunk is used for this craft. The piece is rubbed until it has a soft, warm glow and is not only exciting to touch, but is lovely to look at from all directions. The *kobu* is in many ways related to what we called "feelies," or hand sculptures in modern design classes in the 1960s and 1970s.

But *kobus* were not the only form of work in wood. Many men worked on the carving of representational sculptures, and made small boxes and cabinets. Of special interest were the signs made to give individuality to the doors of the barracks. These varied from wood carvings to displaying wire and rope designs displayed on wood surfaces. Each expressed the families and the people living within that barracks.

While it appeared that the men were more involved in the creating of wood objects, it should be stressed that there was no gender division in the production of crafts. Needlework was a popular craft, and a Mr. Nagahama, who was a traditional master of embroidery, began to teach classes in the Heart Mountain Center in Wyoming. Apparently this was one of the most well attended classes, because Eaton reports that " . . .at one time more than six hundred and fifty pupils were enrolled, and special exhibitions of needlework were being held as established features of the arts and adult education program." Even

Drawing by Mine Okubo from Citizen 13660 *showing an internee at one of the many art exhibitions held at the relocation camps. Courtesy of Mine Okubo.*

though this seemed to be such a well-received and practical handicraft, Eaton utilized only a small number of examples in his book.

Calligraphy was also a very important technique practiced in all the camps. It is a highly traditional art form found in Japan, and the masters of this art are held in high esteem by Japanese and Japanese-Americans. The results of fine calligraphy are usually hung in the *tokonoma*, accompanying a simple and carefully designed flower arrangement.

Other handicrafts, such as painting, rock polishing, drawing, and sculpting from natural branches and stones, were also found in all the relocation centers.

Eaton was extremely excited about the fact that many exhibitions were held in the various camps. His interest in exhibiting handicrafts and art went back to his days in San Francisco and Buffalo, as did his involvement in bringing an awareness of immigrant and native arts to the attention of the American public. He was firmly convinced that through handicrafts, a visual language could be spoken which would help erase the prejudices which were running rampant in this country.

By 1948, Eaton reports in his Christmas letter that he had made considerable progress in his two books in process: *The Art of Japanese in Our War Relocation Camps*, and *Objects of Beauty for the Blind*. With his New England book behind him, he was able to concentrate on his other projects, but because his fame as an expert in handicrafts had grown, he again was interrupted on his work with the two yet-unfinished books.

Early in the summer of 1950, he was invited by the West German government to become a member of a mission of Americans, sponsored by the Economic Co-operation Administration of the Marshall Plan which would travel to Germany to help study the problems of refugees in that country. As a special advisor on Handicrafts and Small Industries, he left the United States for the first time to go to Europe. John Kenneth Galbraith was also a member of the commission.

On his return from Germany, he again settled in to finish *Beauty Behind Barbed Wire*, and in his Christmas letter of 1951, Eaton was excited that the book would be published on February 19, 1952, ten years to the day after the Executive Order was issued authorizing the relocation of the Japanese-Americans. Eaton apparently had worked very hard during 1951, and he writes in the letter,

> *I will have to reserve for another time much that I would like to say here of the wonderful cooperation I have had this year 1951 on* Beauty Behind Barbed Wire, *but I must mention the experience with Gene and Olive Johnson with whom I have been boarded and almost lodged since April until now, working many nights until 1-2-3 and twice even later in the morning. They are of Norwegian blood —fine Americans —and just irregular enough in their habits*

to suit me fine: and Olive's matchless contributions to the work I never can praise enough —I would like to write a little book on her warm understanding, her integrity and her durability. They live about a mile and a half over the hill from us.

In the same letter, Eaton lists what he thinks the book accomplishes:

1. It records one of the most remarkable chapters in the long history of the human arts. 2. It gives briefly but fully enough the story and the explanation of the greatest wrong our government ever did a group in our population, by denying 70,000 citizens the rights guaranteed to every citizen by our Constitution. 3. It shows the fine and loyal qualities of the group of our population which has been most maligned, and most underestimated. 4. It shows convincingly for the first time, I think, how people from the Orient can become worthy and understanding citizens of our democracy, and it suggests what I believe to be true, that America has much to gain from the traditions and culture of the Orient. 5. And last but not least, this is perhaps the most convincing demonstration we have ever had of the greatest quality of our democracy, its political elasticity, that is, the superb fact that when our government makes an error or does a wrong to a group in its population, every citizen is free, and every group is free to help in whatever ways they can to correct that mistake or right that wrong. This is part of what I think of the book, and if it takes another eight years for me to recover what I have had to put into it, you will not hear me complain providing the book does get around. If its worth is discovered, it may return the outlay soon.

The publishing of *Beauty Behind Barbed Wire* was not, however, as easy as it appeared from Eaton's letters. Because Eaton did not have adequate funds, he approached several agencies for aid. He also was having difficulties finding a publisher. Harper & Brothers showed an interest, but only if Eaton could show that the book would have guaranteed sales. Eventually Eaton did receive financial backing for his work from The Rockefeller Foundation, and the Rockefeller Archivist, J. William Hess writes,

> *The Foundation's records have not been opened for research for the years after 1941. However, I can report on actions during the later period. Mr. Eaton first contacted the Foundation about his Japanese art project in September 1947. He was told the Foundation would provide modest support for the project if he could get assurance that publication would be possible. There was a long delay while Mr. Eaton tried unsuccessfully for backing from a commercial or university press. Eventually, the Society for Japanese Studies agreed to sponsor the book and Harper & Brothers agreed to publish it. On March 30, 1951, Foundation officers approved a grant in aid of $3,000 (about $20,000 in 2003 dollars) to the Society for Japanese Studies for preparation of the book on the art of the Japanese relocation camps. Of this grant, approximately $2,400 (about $19,000) was to be used to provide living expenses for Mr. Eaton during eight months of work on the volume and $600 (about $4,800) was to be used for travel, secretarial assistance, etc. The Foundation sent a check for $3,000 to the Society with a cover letter dating April 12, 1951.*

Mr. George W. Jones, Eaton's editor at Harper & Brothers, wrote,

I liked Allen Eaton. He was both a gentleman and a very gentle man. Yet he had a quality of a bull dog persistence where his work was concerned. I am thinking of the way he finally secured the assistance of the Japan Society and obtained from them an order for copies of Beauty Behind Barbed Wire *sufficient to justify its publication by a commercial publisher which it certainly was. His dedication to his chosen field of handicrafts was complete . . .*

With *Beauty Behind Barbed Wire*, as with many of his other books, Eaton became a strong force in distributing copies and promoting sales. Often he published small flyers with information about the book, and with excerpts from different reviews. His Christmas letters usually carried information to his relatives and friends. He very often had several thousand copies of the books delivered to his house where he distributed them as orders came in from around the country. For *Beauty Behind Barbed Wire*, he issued a two-page flyer which had 22 excerpts from reviews and from letters that he had received, many from prominent citizens who were well-aware of Oriental culture. Pearl Buck wrote, "Nothing, perhaps nothing, could reveal to Western eyes the true depth and grace of an ancient Eastern people as this book does . . .(it is) a simple story in its telling, but how profound in its revelation . . . beauty for the eyes; meaning for the mind; and a torch for the spirit." The former Ambassador to Japan, Joseph Grew, wrote, "Its real importance is helping our people to a better understanding of the Japanese and their finer qualities which we understood so intimately during our long stay in Japan." Eaton's friend Mrs. J. Randolph Coolidge wrote, "Your text dimmed my eyes often."

Beauty For The Sighted And The Blind

While they were saying among themselves 'it cannot be done' it was done.

Helen Keller

The Surf Rider *sculpture in the Hall of Man by Malvina Hoffman, The Field Museum (Chicago), Neg. #MH71A.*

*B*eauty for the Sighted and the Blind, Eaton's last book, was not published until 1959, three years before his death. However, it was the result of many years of work, and brings together all his ideas and philosophic thoughts about beauty, art and the handicrafts.

The idea for this work originated during an experience he had while observing a group of blind persons in a small store near his home in the 1930s. He was intrigued as they ran their hands over Christmas merchandise and explored the various goods available for purchase. It was after he discovered that the owner of this store allowed groups of blind people to examine wares and displays that Eaton realized that most blind people do not have opportunities to really enjoy "looking" at beautiful things.

As he became involved in his thoughts about this minority group, he started preliminary research into the possibility of a collection of beautiful art and handicraft objects for the blind to experience through feeling them in a public exhibition. He found that such an endeavor had not been done before on a national or large scale. However, in some progressive schools for the blind, some work had been done in this area.

With his ideas beginning to jell in the winter of 1931, he began. His daughter Elizabeth, who was very interested in and intrigued by the project, donated some of her time to the research. It would be 28 years before the finished written work was published; all his many other projects kept him busy enough, so this idea simply gestated among other concerns during those long years. Many years of the research took place while he was with the Russell Sage Foundation, but Glenn, Brandt, and Andrews devote only a small comment concerning it in their book about the Foundation and its many projects. It was not until 12 years after their book was published by the Foundation that Eaton saw his book come into print.

The foreword by Helen Keller is a touching and meaningful opening to the book. She expresses the importance of such a book and its purpose to encourage:

> *. . .more and happy communications between the sighted and the blind. He affords an impressive, concrete realization of life that will enrich the blind and discard the remoteness which used to be their lot. In his exhibits and the information they spread among the public Mr. Eaton will build up the delightful subjects of common interest between the blind and their seeing fellow.*

The essential goals of the book are four-fold. One is to bring about an awareness of the philosophic aspect of beauty and its relationship to the blind; another is to illustrate the great and potential capabilities of the blind in creating and performing acts of creation; a third is to describe the collection of objects for the exhibition he assembled; and the last is to examine ways in which public agencies could serve the blind and act as stimuli for more communications between the sighted and the blind.

Eaton did much reading and research in order to support the ideas for his exhibition, and to give a better understanding of the problems in his book. He disagreed with the work of Dr. G. Revensz, a highly regarded Dutch author, who had written in his 1950 book *Psychology and the Art of the Blind*: "The loss of vision does not render the practices of plastic art impossible. But finding aesthetic pleasure in works of art, and for creation of new form, sight is essential." Eaton was very opposed to Revensz's position, and felt that instead of helping to bridge the gap between sighted and blind persons, it in fact retarded any understanding. Eaton states in his book that he had heard the comment from blind people for many years, "We who are blind are just like you, except that we do not see with our eyes," and he was convinced that a blind person could enjoy aesthetic experiences as well as a sighted person if given an opportunity.

Eaton includes a chapter titled "Some Abilities and Achievements of Blind Persons," and purposefully uses examples of people who are not artists, but who have excelled in other fields

A. Robinson, a sightless woodsman chopping a tree. Photo by United Press International. Courtesy of Elizabeth and Martha Eaton.

that would appear to be closed to a blind person. Among his selections are a doctor, a minister, a ham radio operator, and a man who built his own house completely by himself. During the research for his book and exhibit, he discovered a small publication called *Beauties and Achievements of the Blind* written by William Artman and L.V. Hall, two young graduates of the New York Institution for the Blind. Eaton felt, as they did, that through education of the public, many misunderstandings could be erased and more understanding built.

The *Collection of Objects of Beauty* which he gathered for the exhibition developed over many years, each year bringing new additions for the exploration by the blind. While some of the items were a part of his personal collection, many were on loan to him. In the final selection of the objects that would become part of the collection, four criteria were considered. The first was that each piece should be beautiful and aesthetic to the sighted person choosing the piece, and that texture, form and color were to be important elements of the object. Even though the blind might not be able to perceive color, it should be an essential ingredient for those who were sighted. Eaton and his assistants felt that the objects should give real enjoyment, interest and pleasure also to those able to see the piece.

Second, the objects should be easily and comfortably held in the hand for examination. Size was a consideration, but as Eaton points out, he was rather surprised to find that the blind person was able to obtain great pleasure from very small objects.

The third consideration was that the object should be able to be handled again and again without damage taking place, and that it should appear as fresh and pleasant for the hundredth person as for the first.

The final and fourth criterion was that the object be limited to the arts of man. No object from nature would be included, but if this exhibit was successful, he already had ideas to have a combined exhibit of the arts of man in combination with objects from nature.

*Babylonian clay tablet from Mesopotamia. Photo by
George Dales, University of Pennsylvania Museum.
Courtesy of Elizabeth and Martha Eaton.*

Parts of his experiments and exhibits were to be executed
and constructed at the Kansas Rehabilitation Center for the
Blind in Topeka, Kansas.

The search for objects was held in many locations. The hunt
took place in New York City, at home, in shops and galleries and
in local antique emporiums. Even though the search was hap-
hazard and intermittent, as Eaton stated, the collection grew
into a workable group of articles which related nicely to each
other. The collection grew to have almost 50 pieces, but this
number changed as new things were added and others deleted
for various reasons. All the pieces had been created by sighted
people, but selected for the enjoyment and touch of the blind.

Included in the collection were a prehistoric hand tool of
stone, a Babylonian clay tablet from Mesopotamia, ceramics,

wood carvings, silver jewelry, *kobu*, scrimshaw, alabaster carving and glass. The objects represented the countries of Japan, Russia, Egypt, China, Denmark, Australia, France, and, of course, the United States. The collection held a real interest for the blind who had an opportunity to "view" it, and Eaton felt that it was the most challenging exhibition that he had ever accumulated in that it demanded more imagination and skill in selection than any other exhibits.

Throughout the chapter concerning the collection of the exhibit, he talks about the reasons and purpose behind each selection:

> *One reason for choosing a basket by an American Indian is that the finest baskets in the history of the human race have been made by our Indians, and some of them in the memory of people still living. This fact also was reason for giving both the sighted and the blind opportunities to see fine examples of Indian handicrafts, and to learn that the present standard of production among tribes is better than it was twenty-five years ago. So a Pomo Indian Ceremonial basket, possibly a gift for a bride, was selected for our collection.*

Many objects came from museums, and many were gifts from various people, both unknown and famous.

> *Then the thought came; perhaps the great maestro Toscanini, would have a baton he would lend us. It was worth trying, especially because of what it would mean to some of the blind friends so fond of music . . . Toscanini, although not well, was happy to send one of his batons for our collection, not as a loan, but as a gift. When it arrived, it had a very special interest for me because of its appearance. It was so simple compared to the different types of batons I have seen at close range in music stores, and sometimes*

Ming ceramic vase. Photo by A. Burton Carnes.
Courtesy of Elizabeth and Martha Eaton.

at longer range in the hands of an orchestra
conductor . . . Toscanini's baton added three new
materials to our collection. The slender pointer was
shaped from a piece of birch; the light handle was of
cork; and the ferrules, or small bracelets supporting
the cork handle, and giving the baton a little color,
were of moss green and coral plastic.

A lacquered Russian box was one interesting object which
found its place into the collection through a blind friend of
Eaton's. His friend suggested that such a box be included, but
many times Eaton had rejected this kind of item because he felt
it was more visual than tactile. It was only after he had listened

to his friend describe the box that he realized he was allowing his visual preference to overweigh the sense of touch in holding such a beautiful textured shape in the hands.

In Eaton's 1944 Christmas letter he mentions the progress being made on this project.

> *I will not take the time and space here to note progress on other Foundation projects, except to say that all my hopes for the 'Exhibition of Objects of Beauty for the Blind' are being confirmed by our experiments with the blind, and it seems certain that this exhibition, and others that follow, will open a door to a new and beautiful world for many sightless people. Our experiments will be completed during the year and probably a small publication describing the experiments printed. It is the most interesting exhibition that I have ever assembled, between forty and fifty fine examples of handiwork from North and South America, Europe, Asia and Africa, including a score of countries, beautiful articles made by white, black, red, yellow, and brown craftsmen from at least a dozen different materials. One of the oldest objects is a Babylonian clay tablet, a written receipt for a few head of sheep incised and burned about 3000 B.C., lent by the Metropolitan Museum of Art; the newest, a pretty example of industrial art, a spiral bracelet of plastic, elastic enough to fit most any hand, purchased at the 'five and ten' store. Each object in size can be comfortably held in one or both hands. Sometime during the year I believe my deep conviction will have been proved, that the blind have within their reach a kingdom of beauty inexhaustible in the longest life-time.*

The experiments that he conducted were held over a long period of time. His friend Louise Pitman tells about his experiments at the Asheville, North Carolina Fair in 1955.

A carved wooden rooster. Photo by A. Burton
Carnes. Courtesy of Elizabeth and Martha Eaton.

He took some blind people through some of the exhibitions here in Asheville. He didn't have his collection here, but he sat them down at a table—two or three mornings during the Fair week at nine o'clock—before the Fair opened. We set up a table and he had already gone through the exhibition and picked out items that he wanted to show. He sat at the head of the table, and the blind people with their escorts were all around. He talked about these things; who made them and so-forth. And then they were passed around the table and everyone felt them. It certainly was a beautiful sight. We tried to keep it out of the newspapers, but the reporters found out about it. He wanted it a private affair.

Eaton tells about the experience in his Christmas letter for that year in different words:

And now to one of my highest experiences of the year, or many years, showing the Craftsmen's Fair to two small groups of blind persons. Louise Pitman, Clementine Douglas and Mrs. Marjorie McClune, an educator for the blind, in Asheville, herself blind, made the preliminary arrangement by which we carried out this pioneer experiment all the details of which we have not space for here; but it included showing quite thoroughly, about a dozen objects selected from the exhibition for their beauty, interest and variety and their size. Each object could be held in one or both hands and examined leisurely through the sense of touch. The guests were seated on the long sides of a ten foot table, each with a sighted companion who would pass the object on as it went around the table for a careful and detailed observation.

The objects were among the best of their kind in the show and covered a wide range of handicraft expressions. Among the handicrafts which I remembered was a sleeping cat from the John C. Campbell Folk School carved from buckeye wood; a piece of stoneware, and also a highly glazed piece of pottery; a double weave Indian basket of river cane, nearly finished, which showed how the weaving was done; a rooster whittled from wood by a woman who tied her model to a post of her front porch to get her carving as life-like as possible; a dulcimer, the original mountain musical instrument made in Kentucky and on which Lynn Gault played an accompaniment for a short mountain ballad; a nice shopping bag, hand woven by Mrs. Maples of Gatlinburg whose eight daughters are all good weavers; a corn husk angel for a Christmas tree decoration, made by Mrs. Burns of Hindman Settlement School; the wood carving of my skunk family, a mother and her five kittens, which Uncle William Martin of Murphy made for me; a fine wild honeysuckle vine basket woven by Mrs. Denton who at 83 demonstrated every day at the Fair; a bob cat which Amanda Crowe, a Cherokee Indian girl and talented sculptor, had partly finished, very rough from hatchet and chisel marks, and fox which she carved of wild cherry, completed with the smoothest possible finish; lovely to the eye, but lovelier through the sense of touch; and other objects beautiful to see and to feel.

Each object was described and interesting facts about it were told before and while it was being passed around; and all had the time they wanted to see it thoroughly. A surprise, for all of us, came through one of the volunteer helps at the Fair, Mrs. King, who had brought a large and beautiful rose geranium plant for my table. She raises geraniums and other scented plants; and on the days when our blind friends came in, she had generous sprays of two of the loveliest fragrances, rose geranium and lemon verbena, for each of them to take home.

*I was told that the Craftsmen's Fair was the subject
of conversation for days, in their homes; one made a
little basket for me as a gift, another wrote a fine letter
of appreciation for opening these vistas of beauty and
the arts for her and other blind people; and another
sent word that this was the most wonderful day she
had ever had . . . .*

Eaton spent many hours conducting experiments with various blind people in anticipation of gaining the insight he wanted
to better understand the problems and aesthetic abilities of the
blind. He worked extensively with the Rehabilitation Center in
Topeka, Kansas and with the North Carolina Museum of Art in
Raleigh, North Carolina.

As usual, Eaton was in need of funds for his many projects,
and since his days at the Russell Sage Foundation were over,
it was much more crucial to obtain backing. His biggest and
most encouraging push came from Mary E. Switzer, who was
director of the Office of Vocational Rehabilitation with the U.S.
Department of Health, Education and Welfare. Eaton applied
for funds through the American Foundation for the Blind and
was rewarded with a research fellowship in the amount of
$19,750. Although this did not come all in one package, it did
extend from May 1954 until June 1958. Some of this money was
designated for the purchase of objects; part was earmarked for
research; and still other dollars were for the specific publication
costs with St. Martin's Press. But with the help of even more
money from the American Foundation for the Blind and a grant
of $10,000 from the Mary Duke Biddle Foundation, Eaton
managed to obtain a total of $33,500 for his project.

When the book finally came off the press, Eaton was not in
the United States, but was totally preoccupied with his trip to
India. In his 1959 Christmas letter, which was the shortest he
had ever written, and written in flight to India, he only mentions that the book would probably be out by now as he headed
for the Far East.

Beauty for the Sighted and the Blind was written as a way to bridge the artistic understanding between sighted people and sightless people. Eaton saw no difference between the blind and the non-blind in his conviction that beauty was, and needed to be, a part of each person's life. He rejected any talk about the fact that sightless people could not enjoy and experience the visual arts in their own way. His first chapter is dedicated to presenting a philosophic belief about beauty that was developed from decades of experience in the arts, and is coupled with the writings and observations of artists, philosophers, and scientists. There is little which is homey or romantic in this book compared to the style that can be found in his other books. These people were not members of social groups which were economically deprived or discriminated against because of their heritage or cultural background. These were simply people without sight who had every other physical faculty available to them and therefore could be as successful in society as any other person if they were given an opportunity to do so.

The philosophic approach and writing style that Eaton takes seem to be pointed not only to the blind, but to a universal understanding of beauty, art and aesthetics for all people. He uses many quotes from many different sources, sometimes citing the title of his source, but often simply reflecting on a particular person's thoughts. Eaton was a collector of quotes, and kept a scrapbook of favorite sayings and ideas which stimulated him.

A few quotes from his chapter on "Beauty: The Aesthetic Experience" will give an insight into Eaton's thinking in his last years:

> *Beauty is first of all a personal, subjective experience; therefore in some form or forms it is probably an experience of every human being . . . it can not be conferred upon one individual by another by wishing or by insisting . . . An aesthetic experience of beauty in nature or the arts cannot be other than an individual reaction to a stimulus . . . Somebody may*

> *ask why the term 'beauty' was chosen to designate*
> *this collection instead of 'art' or 'arts.' The answer*
> *is that beauty is a better understood term, is less*
> *controversial, and had a definitely pleasure giving*
> *connotation.*

He quotes Emerson, "Beauty must come back to the useful and the distinction between fine and useful arts be forgotten." Eaton called further on many other authors who have dealt with beauty and aesthetics in a philosophic and psychological manner. From the psychologist Thomas Cutsforth: "Aesthetic growth does not take place so much through the senses as it does through the entire intellectual development. Aesthetic appreciation is always related to the wealth of effective relationships it organizes about the stimulus pattern."

From Dr. Alexis Carrel, a scientist:

> *Esthetic sense exists in the most primitive human*
> *beings as in the most civilized. It even survives the*
> *disappearance of intelligence ... The creation of*
> *forms, or of a series of sounds, capable of awakening*
> *an esthetic emotion, is an elementary need of our*
> *nature ... Esthetic activity manifests itself in both*
> *the creation and the contemplation of beauty ...*
> *Beauty is an inexhaustible source of happiness to*
> *those who discover its abode.*

Throughout *Beauty for the Sighted and the Blind* Eaton stresses the importance of all of man's senses, as well as their relationship to the intellectual aspects of human developmental growth and understanding of the arts. Basically he is speaking of handicrafts, but he does depart from a straight handicraft approach when he gives the sightless an opportunity to examine sculptures in the Hall of Man at the Field Museum of Natural History in Chicago. Eaton was not unfamiliar with the fine arts; he had been involved with painting and other art forms from his

Oregon days, but he did see handicrafts as a more useful form of the arts which could bring help to the blind and to others whom he was attempting to help.

Eaton was a pioneer in establishing programs of art appreciation for the blind, although as mentioned earlier, a few private schools for the blind had carried on some experiments in this area. While Eaton had worked primarily with his personal experiments, he did attempt to get several programs introduced into museums. There were few educational programs for sightless people in any museums here in the United States during most of his explorations, but because of his work, the concept was slowly picked up by several institutions.

One such organization that he influenced was the North Carolina Museum of Art in Raleigh, North Carolina. Louise Pitman was disturbed that Eaton was never given credit for much of his pioneer work, and especially that which he inspired in Raleigh:

> *It always irked me that Allen Eaton was never given credit for that. I knew that man who was general curator there and I wrote him and something about why couldn't they give Allen Eaton a little recognition. Well, he referred the letter—as he had to—to the director of the museum at the time, and the man never answered my letter. Eventually he had to retire, but my friend Ben Williams felt that the man didn't give Eaton real recognition. I think he's had a little since.*

The Mary Duke Biddle Education Gallery was opened in 1966 to provide exhibitions designed with attention to the needs of handicapped visitors.

Eaton has never received the real recognition that he should have had for his work in programs for the blind in museums. In a recent publication called *Museums and the Handicapped*, issued by the Smithsonian Institute, Eaton is not mentioned at all, yet Mary Switzer, who had supported his work through financial grants, is cited several times. Also in this publication, the North Carolina Museum of Art is cited as being a pioneer in museum exhibitions for the blind, but Eaton, the real instigator of the program is not mentioned. Very few young craftsmen today know the contributions that Eaton has given to the craft world, and are always surprised at his varied and extensive gifts to American crafts.

Once *Beauty for the Sighted and the Blind* was published while he was on his way to India, Eaton never again mentioned it in his Christmas letters. His interests were quickly diverted to his work on the India handicrafts exhibition.

The Final Years

I pass thru this world but once, any good things therefore that I can do, or any kindness I can show to any human being, let me do it now. Let me not defer it, not neglect it, for I shall not pass this way again.

Found in Eaton's scrap book of quotations, marked author unknown.

Eaton teaching in the 1950s at Arrowmont School of Arts and Crafts. Courtesy of Arrowmont School of Arts and Crafts.

The last years of Eaton's life were not devoted to a quiet time of retirement, an era that began when he left the Foundation in 1946. He continued to work on his books and writings and many other projects the day he stepped out of the Foundation, and he kept looking for new directions and research which placed him in the foreground of the handicrafts and arts movements.

Some of his most delightful times were spent teaching during the summer at the Gatlinburg Workshop, which is now called the Arrowmont School of Crafts. Eaton was enthralled with teaching there and attending the Southern Highland Handicraft Guild Fairs. Many of his students recall his days there in a reverent way. When Eaton first went to Gatlinburg to teach, the school was active but small. The modern craft center building, which now sits above the busy tourist town, was only a spark in the mind of director Marian Heard and the Pi Beta Phi Sorority. The town, at that time, was lazily tucked in the mountain

Eaton at Berea College, Kentucky. Courtesy of Arrowmont School of Arts and Crafts.

along the West Fork of the Little Pigeon River that wandered through the Smoky Mountains. It must have been an idyllic spot for a New Yorker to spend a few thoughtful weeks.

Eaton writes about his experience in his 1948 Christmas letter.

> *Prince is not the only dog that got off his leash and ran away this summer. About the middle of June, I slipped mine, and spent nearly six weeks in the Southern Highlands, an experience I needed, and for which I am deeply thankful. I gave a background course in* Handicrafts in American Life and Culture, *at the Summer Workshop at the Gatlinburg, Tennessee, to a fine group of students from more than thirty states. The Workshop represents the coordinated efforts of the Pi Beta Phi sorority, through their Settlement School, and the University of Tennessee; both organizations made the summer a happy one for me.*

Most of the people who studied with Eaton remember him in different ways. Bernice Stevens speaks of her experiences when she attended his seminars at Gatlinburg as terribly boring, until slowly she became aware of Eaton's knowledge and ability.

> *He wandered around the front of the room, and he talked about this, and he talked about that. It took a long time to realize what he was. I was very unappreciative of him at first. My relationship with him was one that grew as we did things together.*

Marian Heard, who was director of the Workshop, and retired in 1977 from the directorship of Arrowmont, complains about the fact that he wanted to give all the students 'A's. He would say, "Why Marian, they are all such nice girls. I just cannot give them anything less."

Eaton kept up a fairly regular correspondence with Marian Heard. Most often the letters dealt with his work for the approaching summer workshop. Heard was always well-organized in her scheduling of the summer classes, usually having completed the task by December, and not later than January. Only in rare cases did she fall behind in her own personal schedule.

In May 1950, Eaton wrote to her about some of his concerns about working with the students.

> *I have a June 1 deadline for some writing I have been doing, and then comes choosing things and thoughts for the Workshop in addition to the ideas that have been floating in ever since you called me.*

> *I will not undertake here to outline what I have in mind, but the main points will be encouragement for worthy works in all the arts; and a new effort to bring out in our students their potentialities and encourage them to share their best experiences with their companions of a few weeks.*

> *I will try to get my exhibit up earlier, and it will help if one assistant could be assigned earlier. Maybe my getting there early myself will help this.*

On February 3, 1951, Eaton wrote Heard concerning his problem of not being able to commit himself to coming to Gatlinburg for the summer.

> *I am sure you know, without my telling you, how disappointed I was and am to be unable to come to a favorable conclusion about the Workshop in time. I have always been indefinite, but this year it has been harder than ever because of complications with which I won't trouble you, and the pressure of getting out the 'Arts of the Japanese in Our War Relocation Camps,' if it is humanly possible to do it. I could*

finish it alright, but it looks as though I would have to practically sponsor it—at least raise the money for it. I can do this if the Guggenheim Fellowship comes through, but will not know until March . . . I know you will understand—as you always do—and I do not have to tell you how disappointed I am. My one consolation is the money I would make can probably be used to good advantage in this time of universal budget cutting.

If I ever get a few days off I will try to let you know how very much the association with the Workshop, with you and our dear associates has meant to me, so much that I must leave it largely to your imagination—but it will always be one of my greatest privileges. Remember me to each one as you can.

Affectionately, Allen Eaton

In addition to traveling to Gatlinburg for teaching the summer workshops, Eaton also traveled during the summers to attend fairs. He was a constant guest at the Southern Highland Handicraft Guild Fair, usually helping with getting exhibitions in place. He was not above doing the last-minute sweeping of the floors, or taking out the trash. He contributed all his strength and interest in each fair he attended, much to the joy of the craftspeople.

The late O.J. Mattil talked about AE's involvement with the Gatlinburg and Asheville Fair:

Oh—he often exhibited things with the Fair and the Guild. He was very interested in the Fair, and he continued with the Fair. He helped us a great deal when it was here in Gatlinburg for three years, and then when it went to Asheville. Later when we didn't use him so much, I think he missed a couple of years—when he didn't come down. And when he did come down, we used him more or less to talk to

Allen Eaton on his Germany consulting trip with unidentified woman. Courtesy of Elizabeth and Martha Eaton.

*people for special activities on the stage. We set up his
background for him. Clem Douglas did—and others
worked with him also. He did that India exhibit, and
then another thing he did—he was very interested in
the blind. And then he and those people met with him.
He took them around and had them feel of things.*

Eaton had been attending the fairs in New Hampshire since
they were first instigated, and now with the Southern Highland
Handicraft Guild Fair, beginning in 1948, he had two to attend,
and he seldom missed either of them. In 1948, he writes about
the Gatlinburg Fair.

*For some time I had been urging the Southern
Highland Handicraft Guild and the Highlanders, to
hold in the Appalachia area, a regional Craftsmen's
Fair, similar to those which have done so much for the
handicraft movement in New Hampshire in recent
years. Toward the end of July, following the summer
Workshop, they held their first Fair at Gatlinburg;
so I stayed on to see it, and do what I could to help.
My special job was to look after the photographing,
and we got a fine record of the event. The Fair was
held in the stone building of the Settlement School,
on the green, and under eight or nine large tents. It
was carefully planned, well managed and visitors
were thrilled with it. The exhibition of mountain
handicrafts was beautiful and comprehensive. The
sales rooms were so tastefully arranged that they were
exhibitions in themselves, and all the managers of the
six Highland Shops came in and ran the business.*

At this first fair there were also other arts demonstrated and
exhibited. Ballad singers, folk dancers, musicians, and puppe-
teers all captured the essence of the mountain people and their
arts. Eaton was thrilled with it as he mentioned in his 1948

Eaton with Brasstown Carvers, July 14, 1947.
Courtesy of Elizabeth and Martha Eaton.

Christmas letter, for it made him think back 28 years to the *Arts and Crafts of the Homelands* exhibit.

Eaton also made an annual pilgrimage to New Hampshire to visit the League of New Hampshire Fair. He was always interested in seeing his friends in every place he revisited. He was a frequent visitor to the Pennsylvania Guild of Arts and Crafts (now called the Pennsylvania Guild of Craftsmen) Fairs as well, because he had been instrumental in getting that organization off the drawing boards in 1940. He wrote about staying with the Osborns, in their small comfortable home in the center of Pennsylvania. Milton Osborn had been very active in the early stages of getting the Pennsylvania Guild started.

In the summer of 1950, Eaton was invited to participate in a study of German Handicrafts and Small Industries by the Economic Co-Operation Administration. He was 72 years of age, but still an active and eager "young man", and he accepted the job with ardor, even though he was hesitant because of his lack of knowledge of the German language. The mission, which was organized by Hans Christian Sonne of New York, was based on previous fact-finding data prepared by the Congressional "Macy Committee," and was part of the Marshall Plan for European Recovery. Sonne was chairman of the commission.

After the team of ten members went to Washington D.C. for a briefing about Germany and the refugee problem, they sailed to Europe in September for a three-month stay. Most of the time was spent in Germany, but Paris was on the itinerary as well. Eaton did not write a great deal about his work in Germany, but he did include part of the Introduction to the report which was turned over to the German government in his 1950 Christmas letter. He felt that the report was confidential and could not be released until after the German government had an opportunity to review it. The Introduction pointed out the great need for cultural integration of native Germans and refugees as a beginning to economic reconstruction.

He points out in the letter what handicrafts were in Germany at the time of his visit.

> *Incidentally—handicrafts in Germany includes all the trades and professions doing hard work, almost everything up to mass production industry, and it is in the handicraft field, especially, where independent and experienced refugees have been able to get their new start in work and life. Already the refugees have established 38,335 new industries in western Germany, employing 112,000 people, and they have started them in prison camps, in barracks, munitions works and other places usually considered unfit for human habitation. It is this combined process of industry and integration that is the hope of Germany today. Happily, as I have pointed out in the report, the refugee was conscious that integration is a cultural, as well as an economic process. The problem is a much greater one than is realized by many of the German population . . . .*

Eaton was very concerned about the integration facet as a cultural, social and economic need, which reflected his philosophy about immigrants and the Japanese-Americans in this country. He was consistently aware of the Americanization process that we have in the United States, and that while this integration must take place in terms of groups of people being accepted as a part of a society, he felt they must at the same time retain their individual heritages as part of their lifestyle. This was a concept well advanced for its time.

During the 1950s Eaton continued to travel, visiting the various craft fairs and collecting various materials for different projects he had in mind to finish some day in the future. Retirement and freedom from a specific job gave him the flexibility he seemed to need so much. In 1952, he headed west to visit Eugene, Oregon, and attended the 50th reunion of his class at the University. He spent time seeing his relatives on both sides of the family, and making pilgrimages to the small home he had left in 1918. He renewed his friendships in Portland, La Grande, Union, Salem and Eugene.

Beauty Behind Barbed Wire had just been published and he felt he could spend a leisurely summer building up a final file of his memories. While he was in Oregon he gave several talks to the University summer school and did some research at the University archives concerning Deadly Hall, the building in which his father-in-law had been so interested.

> *This renewal of relationship with the University and with the town of Eugene—now the city—was a happy event in more ways than I can say; but I had a mixed feeling about it which I suppose no one can understand and I do not think I can adequately describe. I felt, and still feel, that I am as much a part of the future of the town and of the University as I am a part of the past.*

These comments in his 1952 Christmas letter are so much an indicator of the man he was—unable to hold grudges, and always looking on the good side of everything. He closes his letter that year with some commentary of his woodpile activities.

> *There is room—if you have time—for one of the twenty stories of my 1952 woodpile. I did cut cedar log the other night as I told you I aimed to do. It was late dusk when I got to the woodpile, and as I sawed away, releasing the fragrant wood dust in the cool night air, the lovely evening star in the east the only witness, dimly I heard coming out of the sky to the South, the honk of wild geese, and in a few seconds Akka and forty three of his flock, in the V shape they always take, flew bound for St. Eleanor's Lake, as I know from their turning soon after. They need not*

Above: Eaton and Mme. Kamaladevi Chattopadhyay (to his right) examining craft books presented to the All-India Handicraft Board, by American publishers. Courtesy of Elizabeth and Martha Eaton. Below: Eaton speaking at opening of New Delhi Craft Museum. Courtesy of Elizabeth and Martha Eaton.

have flown over us at all; they could have saved time
and missed us as they usually do; I think this excursion
was just to give me something special to write about.
Anyway I have been thinking of it ever since, and
what ever the reason or lack of it, the spectacle of
the evening star, the flight of the wild geese, the
fragrance of cedar wood, the ring of a crosscut saw,
the promise of a sweet-smelling wood box all winter
and good wood to burn, and thoughts of you—isn't
that something even if it can't be reasoned out?

In 1955, Eaton made a journey to Sante Fe, New Mexico
where Robert Hart, formerly of the Southern Highlands, but
then of the Indian Arts and Craft Service, met him and " . . .did
everything that could be done to make my stay what it should
be." Eaton loved the Indian crafts of the Southwest, and was
terribly moved when he visited Mesa Verde, spending almost
the whole night watching the landscape change through star-
light and moonglow.

It seemed that Eaton's travels multiplied the older he grew.
His next big opportunity came in 1959 when the Ministry of
Social Welfare in Barbados invited him to prepare a preliminary
survey of handicrafts of that island and the Windward Islands.
The mission was sponsored by the International Cooperation
Administration.

He spent two weeks exploring various possible ways in which
Barbados could enrich its handicraft program, searching for
handicrafts which might make a stronger contribution to economic development. In a letter which Eaton wrote from the
Ocean View Hotel in Bridgetown, he saw such possibilities for
coordination of handicraft interests among the Leeward and
Windward islands that,

I hope I can persuade them to undertake a four or
five year programme to explore and develop these
possibilities which I am certain can bring results

*beyond their present dreams. I am staying a few days
longer to attend the 'Annual Exhibition' of the Island.
They tell me that everything which people grow and
make will be shown without screening, and that is
just what I want to see. Already I have found some
very interesting and worthy handicrafts which are
not known to my colleagues here which I know will
fascinate many an island visitor if he can find them.*

Allen Eaton was intrigued with the people, as he always was
when he traveled. He constantly talked with the people on the
streets, in the stores, and in the fields, because here he could
learn about them and their heritage. He especially enjoyed
watching the young women in Barbados carrying large loads of
goods on trays on their heads. "I am hoping to see, before I go,
a neighbor of one of the young women in the Ministry of Social
Welfare who carries a pail of water on her head for more than
a mile riding a bicycle. There is nothing about this stunt that
depresses anybody. It is admirable and one of the most graceful
actions I have seen."

His next opportunity to travel came to him through an
invitation from the Department of Commerce to prepare an
exhibition of handicrafts for the World Agricultural Fair to be
held in New Delhi, India in 1960. He was contacted late in the
previous summer, which only gave him a few months to collect examples of American handicrafts and get them packed
and loaded on the boat for India. The task was formidable,
to say the least, but Eaton, in his 81st year, was not afraid to
tackle the large and complex job. Because the invitation came
during the summer, Eaton immediately contacted the many
fairs being held around the country in order to get the type of
objects he wanted to represent the American crafts in India.
Eaton was already being called "The Dean of American Crafts,"
and no craftsman could refuse to respond to a man who was so
well-known and so well-liked in the field. And the craftsmen
were pleased to have their work exhibited in another country,

which gave them international recognition. In a short time Eaton managed to collect 1,000 objects.

But his problems had just begun. During the time that Eaton was collecting crafts, he heard from Washington that because of a shortage of money, the craft part of the Fair might need to be cancelled or abandoned altogether. Eaton was shocked.

> *I couldn't believe it. It just didn't seem right. This was the first time, I thought, we had good judgment to use crafts as a medium of communication. This is what I had been wishing and working for for so many years. To my mind, if the show was successful it might influence the State Department to do more with crafts in its future programs. I couldn't let the project die, and I couldn't let the craftsmen down. So after a round of correspondence with Washington, we pushed on and finally got the main shipment off to India.*

Eaton then discovered there would be no one in India to help install the collection, so again he tackled Washington. This time he went to Washington using his own funds to push for an assistant to help him. Finally he was given approval to have a helper; he selected Gerald Williams, a potter from New Hampshire, who not only had lived in India as a child, but knew Hindi as well. But after that the total plans were withdrawn by Washington, and Eaton had to attack the administration again. He was finally reinstated, but as an individual and not as an official member of the Fair. At the last minute, according to a report in the May-June 1960 issue of *Craft Horizon*, clearance for both Williams and Eaton was withdrawn, leaving them no space on the government-chartered planes which were going to India. With typical perseverance, Eaton collected money from friends, booked a flight to India, and he and Williams took off.

They arrived in New Delhi only to discover that they had been ousted from the main Fair buildings, leaving them only with an open tent and no display units for showing the crafts. They worked diligently putting together an exhibition as best they could, and it was a delight for most of the fair-goers.

Eaton's determination to hold this exhibition and his bombardment of Washington made him persona non grata with administrators in the American government. Besides losing his free ticket for the flight, the facilities for a good exhibition, and government support, he had also lost his Washington connections. But regardless of all the difficulties encountered by Eaton and Williams, the final results were amazing. During the Fair and his stay in India, Eaton gleefully wore the native turban which endeared him to the Indian population, reminiscent of his 1938 experiments with the L.L.D. hood and the B.V.D.'s.

Before Eaton left for India, Clem Douglas had arranged through a loan of several hundred dollars for Eaton to gather some craft objects from India so that an exhibition of Indian crafts could be held at the Southern Highland Handicraft Guild Fair in Asheville. At this small exhibition in Asheville in the summer of 1960, called *Hands Across the Sea*, a two-page flyer was handed out to explain the handicraft exhibition in India, and the exchange show displayed in Asheville. Several Indian students from the University of Tennessee acted as hosts at the exhibit and delighted the annual fair visitors.

The India and Asheville exhibitions made significant moves toward bringing about a better understanding of American and other peoples around the world, even though the United States government did nothing to support the activity in the manner that was planned. While Eaton was in India, he gave several talks, one sponsored by the All-India Handicraft Board. He met Prime Minister Nehru who was the first visitor to sign the guest book at the exhibition which was dedicated to Mahatma Gandhi. According to accounts, this small handicrafts exhibit attracted more attention than did all other exhibits, including the large and comprehensive Soviet Union Hall.

When Eaton left India, he presented a small library of craft books to the All-India Handicraft Board. He was proud of and fulfilled by his accomplishment as he and Gerry Williams returned home via Japan.

⁕

In addition to all of his many activities, Eaton managed to accumulate a large number of friends in the art world. He cherished those friends working anonymously in the mountains of the Southern Highlands, and held their work and character in high regard. He also acquired many others who were famous or became famous. Anna Mary Robertson was one of the latter, who in later years startled the art world with her primitive paintings. Eaton first mentions "Grandma Moses" in his 1940 Christmas letter, relating the fact that she had almost missed the opening of her show because she had to paper some bedrooms for a friend before she went to New York. He was especially pleased to think that he knew her before she was "discovered."

In 1955, he wrote,

I have had two visits with Grandma Moses, in whose honor a fine exhibition of her paintings is in place in New York for the month of December at 12 East 57th Street. Our first and longest visit was at Eagle's Bridge, New York, her home, soon after her 95th birthday. Our next, a short one, just after Thanksgiving, in New York, where she told me she had painted three pictures recently; subjects: "September," "October," and "November," and she was going right on with the other nine months of the year, which she can do anytime for she paints them out of her imagination. I knew Grandma before she was discovered, first seeing some of her paintings in the drug store at Hoosick Falls. I helped with some of the details in her first exhibition here. And I was at her second exhibition at Gimbel's Department Store, when she came down from the country and, at the opening, asked that a small table be placed in the

center of it where she unwrapped a newly baked loaf
of bread, a jar of jelly and one of preserves, and put
them on display. She explained that at the County
Fair she had taken prizes for her jams and jellies, but
never any for her paintings ... When I first visited
her on the farm at Eagle's Bridge she was working
on five landscapes that she had lined up; her method
then was to squeeze out of the tubes on the tip of her
brush, a good measure of color, pink for instance, and
one after another, put it on all the pictures which
needed it ...Grandma is little, stooped, and lame,
when standing or walking, but you never notice it
when she is still painting well at 98, and I feel is
growing every year.

Eaton and his daughter Martha visited with Grandma Moses at her home several times during 1960 and 1961, the year in which she died at 101 years of age. He and Martha also took steps to have the school which Grandma Moses attended made into a memorial to her. The school, over a hundred years of age at the time, was one-room. "It is in excellent condition, with the same old bell, and you will hear more about it later. I promise to send, in my next Christmas letter, more thoughts about Grandma Moses, for of all the people I know, none have said more simply and clearly that 'the earth is beautiful: and to live is wonderful'." But Eaton never had an opportunity to finish his treatise about Grandma Moses. The next year he himself died without finishing his 1962 Christmas letter.

From Eaton's earliest years, he was obsessed with Noah's Ark. In the 1915 *Panama-Pacific Exposition*, he exhibited a small wooden ark with all the animals brightly painted, and in following years he continued to collect and look for interesting examples of miniature arks. He often signed his Christmas letters "from the Ark," and considered that the official name of the Eaton residence. In the opening of his 1949 Christmas letter he explains the Ark:

Once upon a time there lived on a great forest of beeches and oaks, ashes, maples, sycamores, hickories, elms, lindens, birches, dogwoods, pines, spruces, hemlocks, cedars, and other trees native to that part of the world, a wood chopper, his wife, their two daughters and their three cats. Their house, if such a habitation could be so called, was of their own design and partly of their own making. Their neighbors referred to it—the nice ones—as the wood chopper's cottage; the others—not so nice—as the wood chopper's hut; but the wood chopper and his family didn't care anyway, because they called it the ark.

They called it 'the ark' because of its shape, and its sturdy build, and because it was designed as much for animals as for men. In case of another flood they believed it would hold together for more than forty days and forty nights and that would be enough; and it had many windows so that the animals could look out and get their minds off their internal troubles, and it had a fireplace before which the mamma hippopotamus could bath her baby with impunity . . .

Eaton loved his home into which he had moved his family in 1929, but he loved his attic even more. Here he did most of his writing and hatching of ideas, and stored his personal things which he had collected over the years. He described his attic to his many friends via the 1947 Christmas letter after he had retired.

It is 7 o'clock in the morning. I am in the attic—to be factual my attic—in our little house in Crestwood sitting in the beautiful yellow writing chair which old Mr. Banning, of Hadlyne, Connecticut made at my request for the Worcester Handicraft Exhibition, a wonderful possession. I have wished for such a chair with writing arm for years, and here it is in one of the best spots on the globe.

My attic is one of the strong bits of evidence which I will use someday to prove that beauty is a subjective experience, as much for the mind as for the eye, and that 'what is one man's meat is another man's poison' as they used to say—and it bothered me a lot as a youngster because of fear that anybody might get some of the poison. What I am aiming to say is that this attic is a wonderful place—Cecile says a 'fearful and wonderful place' and she puts emphasis on fearful while I put it on wonderful, and sometimes when we are emphasizing together a stranger might get any kind of impression. But I tell you it's wonderful for the things that are in it, for the outlook, and especially because it is 'me own'.

1962 was a big year and an industrious one for a man in his 82nd year of life. But Eaton was never one to sit back and rock in his chair, and he stated in his unfinished letter in early December, "Although not intended to be, and much of it all of sudden, the Year 1962 turned out to be one of the best visiting years, starting in the southern highlands in January, and west to Chicago and the Pacific coast in June and July, and few days in New Hampshire in November." It almost appeared that he was touching base with all of his dear friends for the last time.

Allen H. Eaton died on December 7, 1962 on the Crestwood suburban train station platform of an apparent heart attack. It was morning and he was on his way to the New York Public Library where he had been assigned a work space in the Frederick Lewis Allen Memorial Room. As usual he had many projects "cooking." He listed as his current work on the application form for the Library: *The Life and Work of Grandma Moses, The Story of Noah's Ark and the Deluge, The Folk Arts and Handicrafts in American Life and Culture, Handicrafts in the West Indies,* and *The Nubian Project in Egypt* (UNESCO).

A few days after Eaton died, Jerome Nathanson officiated at a memorial service at the New York Society for Ethical Culture. Eaton had long been a member of the Society and was an Honorary Trustee on the Board of Trustees.

Like Grandma Moses, Eaton was a plain person and the following story gives us a perfect insight into his personality, the way he would have loved to have a book about him end.

In 1944, Eaton relates a little story about his favorite bowl. This small yarn-spinning in his Christmas letter tells us much about the humor of Eaton, his simplicity and his love of beauty in all things.

> *And speaking of bowls, I'm planning to have a replica made soon of my favorite old stoneware bowl. Some of you will remember seeing me, or hearing me eating bread and milk from this wonderful bowl designed by Cecile for the Panama Exposition in 1913, I think it was, and used by me up to 1929, when Cecile insisted on giving it to our little fox terrier Cricket to eat out of under the kitchen stove. It was my favorite of all dishes, a sturdy beautiful, oyster white form, convenient to hold in one or both hands, or between the teeth, and the inside of the bowl round to the bottom so that a spoon would fit it perfectly, but wonderful to get into if you didn't happen to have a spoon handy. But I never had the privilege of using it after 1929 because there was always something in it for Cricket; and my family never allowed me to eat Cricket's food; on the other hand Cricket was never permitted to eat anything that I touched. But in the summer when the folks were on vacation I would sometimes exchange bowls with Cricket; but alas one day, when we were eating under the stove together, she tried to take the bowl away from me, and we broke it! That was seven years ago.*

Aileen O. Webb (Aileen Vanderbilt Webb), a board member of The American Craft Council and founder of *Craft Horizon* wrote this as an obituary for the magazine in early 1963.

ALLEN EATON, 1878-1962, often referred to as 'Dean of American Crafts,' died suddenly on December 7. Throughout his years he believed in the necessity and value of the arts and especially of the crafts, in the life of people and communities, and he translated this belief into action as executive and author . . . It was not so much his deeds that endeared him to all who knew him but dedication to his beliefs, his love of beauty, his simpleness of purpose, his clarity in appraising others, and the humbleness and sweetness of his spirit. The world has a need for men like Allen Eaton, and those of us who knew and loved him are richer for the privilege.

Eaton's life was over, but his spirit would continue long after his death.

afterword

Allen H. Eaton at Arrowmont School of Arts and Crafts in his final years. Courtesy of Arrowmont School of Arts and Crafts.

Memorial Service For
Allen H. Eaton
Society For Ethical Culture

Remarks By
Jerome Nathanson
December 12, 1962

Since all of us in this room were Allen Eaton's friends, it surely won't come as any surprise to any of you to know that Allen didn't want a funeral service, and he didn't want a memorial service, and so we haven't met together for Allen Eaton at all, we've met for us, because of our feelings about him, and what he's been in our lives. Allen as you know had innumerable gifts, and he had a very special gift of friendship. And although he lived a long, long life and outlived many of his contemporaries, if all of Allen's friends were to be gathered together, not this room, not three times nor ten times this room could hold that man's friends. It's a strange thing about life that we often think in the course of a lifetime and sometimes even say that every human being is irreplaceable. But of course it's only at the time of death that the full impact of this comes home to us. The Eaton home will be an emptier home, because Pop's not there. The people who have been working with Allen will find it an emptier place. And it will be empty in their hearts. This is true in all the relationships he had.

For many years, as some of you know, he was a trustee of this Society and Secretary of the Society and then Honorary

Trustee. For many years indeed there wasn't a Sunday morning when Allen wasn't sitting right here. And in recent years he didn't feel up to coming with that regularity.

He was a farm boy. Strange to think in this country of ours, how the operations span each other. Allen's father was one of the Oregon pioneers, one of the settlers. When he didn't continue to be a farmer, even though his parents hoped very much he would be, he never lost the sense of what's rural in this increasingly urban society. And as you know this is where so much of his work went.

I've known Allen, not as long as many of you, but I've know Allen for over 25 years. And I thought I knew a great deal about him. I don't think any of you except the most intimate of his friends and his family know what this man really was, what he did. And I'm just going to read to you some of the things in the course of a lifetime that this man did. Just some of them.

He'd been a lecturer in the School of Architecture and Applied Arts at the University of Oregon. He was for over ten years a member of the Oregon legislature in their House of Representatives. He planned and installed the Art Room at the Oregon Building of the *Panama-Pacific Exposition*, the World's Fair of 1915. He has been National Field Secretary for the American Federation of Art. He organized and he directed the Department of Arts and Social Work of the Russell Sage Foundation. He was the Advisor to the United States Department of Agriculture on their Rural Arts program. He organized and directed the first *National Exhibition of Rural Arts*. He was the Advisor of Handicrafts for the International Countrywomen of the World. I think all of you know about the study he made, quite independently, of the art created by the Japanese in that blot on American history, the period of the internment of native Japanese in relocation centers. He was with the ECA Mission to Germany as a government consultant of small industries and handicrafts after World War II. He was with the International Cooperative Administration as a consultant surveying the Barbados and Windward Islands for the Department of the Interior. He assembled the *United States Handicraft Exhibit*, and planned and interpreted it at the first *World Agricultural Fair* in New Delhi, India. He pioneered research on exhibitions of beauty for the blind. And this was his last book.

He had innumerable citations. From the Department of the Interior, from the Department of Commerce. He received honorary degrees from the University of Oregon and from Berea College. When he was awarded the Doctor of Law degree from Oregon, the citation read: "In recognition of his foresight and courage as legislator, citizen and public servant. His tireless endeavor in promoting an appreciation of beauty and art and creative craftsmanship, and his sympathetic and enlightened understanding of the vital contributions which foreign-born citizens have made to the culture and civilization of America." And when he was awarded the degree of Doctor of Humane Letters by Berea College in Kentucky, the citation read: "Student and scholar who has found beauty in the common creations of man and interpreted the arts of mind and hand for the enrichment of life for all." If any human being in my experience ever enriched people's lives, Allen did. There was a gentleness and a sweetness about him that, I think, combined with his being a fighter, a combination of a stiff spine for something in which he believed and this incomparable gentleness and sweetness. I've never experienced this combination in any other human being. The gentle and sweet people, and this is not a criticism of them, as we all know are more rather than less inclined to be soft, to be tender-minded rather than tough-minded. Not Allen. He knew what had to be, he knew what he had to dedicate himself to. He was a person of great courage. And he survived one crisis in his lifetime that I think would have defeated most people. When he felt completely let down by everybody, even the people who loved him most, except his family and a couple of friends, he rebuilt a life in terms of what he was.

Because Allen has not been around the meeting house here so frequently in recent years, I asked a member of our staff yesterday, "Did you know Mr. Eaton?" and his response was,

"Oh, yes, he was a beautiful person!" As a human being, Lord knows he was wonderful to look at, but what came from inside, this was the beauty of it and this was the quality of it. And he had an ability, I don't know how he ever did it, he probably didn't even know himself. When he would talk with people (it happened so many times with me, it must have happened with all of you, it must have happened with endless numbers of people) when Allen talked with you, you felt as if you were more of a person. I don't know how he did it. It made you feel good, that he, this person, thought you were so good, and all the time you knew you weren't that good, so you had an ambivalent feeling. Maybe I can try to be as good as he thinks I am. He made people more of themselves. There's a saying that we quote from Felix Adler, the founder of this movement, perhaps too often: "So act as to elicit the best in other people and thereby in yourself." Well, he was an elicitor of the best, on every level, at all times, and I repeat, with endless people.

He wasn't just a talker. Periodically after Sunday meetings, if in one of the addresses one of us had talked about a particular problem in the city, never mind all the international things, the big things that most of us can only talk about, where you can't really feel effective, Allen would come up to the leader who had spoken that morning and say, "That's a very important problem, and a group in the Society or the community should be organized to deal with the problem. Let's not talk about it, let's do something about it." To make the community and to make the nation something of which one can ever be more proud.

Well, I've talked about affiliations and activity. I'm sure that when Allen suddenly dropped dead on the station platform he was thinking of the new projects he was going to undertake. This man in his 85th year. It was endless. There wasn't time to do what had to be done in this lifetime, after all he did. If he had retired when compulsorily by law he had to retire from the Foundation, he would have had a life work that any human being could have taken endless pride in. Allen couldn't retire. All the materials go into the house. One would expect it. And the work goes on and the new projects start. This is what it was to live, because to live was to create. He belonged to innumerable associations. I have a list here of something like 20 of them. He was a member of the American Pioneer Trails Association, the American Federation of Arts, the Audubon Society, the Early American Industries Association, Microscopical Society, Typophiles, Wildlife Society, Association for the Blind, and so on and so on. But he didn't just belong. Those of you who didn't know the Ethical Society will never know, as members here present well know, including a past President with whom Allen served as Secretary of the Society, that when he belonged to something, he gave himself to it. There wasn't anything that he wouldn't do if he could do it. And this was true with every one of Allen's associations. That's not enough. He wrote all the books and did all the research that went into them. And I think he took pride in them. I hope he did, because they are extraordinary books.

Some of you may be surprised as I was to learn that his first book, instead of being in the field of the arts, was on the Oregon System of Direct Legislation. As long as 50 years ago! Even at that time his field was teaching art appreciation. His books on the *Handicrafts of the Southern Highlands*, the *Handicrafts of New England*, *Beauty Behind Barbed Wire* (that was the Japanese relocation camps), and his last one, *Beauty for the Sighted and the Blind*, are classics and will always remain classics. He had a feeling of it, the taste, the sensitivity that had to be shared. Not just to enjoy but to be shared.

He had this gift for friendship. He was a person of great love. He loved his family very dearly. He had an incomparable marriage for 60 years. That's a lot of marriage. That's a lot of life. That's a lot of love. He was blessed as we were blessed by him. As someone once wrote, "So I be written in the book of love, I do not care about that book above. Erase my name or write it as you will. So I be written in the book of love." Allen's name is there, forever.

b i b l i o g r a p h y

Adamic, Louis. *A Nation of Nations*. New York: Harper and
    Brothers, 1945.

Adams, Ansel. *Born Free and Equal*. New York: U.S. Camera,
    1944.

"Art in Toys." The International Studio 63 (1917): LVIII-LIX.

Bayer, Herbert; Gropius, Ise; and Gropius, Walter. *Bauhaus 1919-*
    1928. New York: Museum of Modern Art, 1938.

Bosworth, Allen R. *America's Concentration Camps*. New York:
    W.W. Norton & Company, Inc., 1967.

Buffalo Fine Arts Academy. *Academy Notes* 14, 1920.

_____. *Art Catalog and Yearbook*, 1920.

Campbell, John C. *The Southern Highlander and His Homeland*.
    New York: Russell Sage Foundation, 1921.

Clark, Robert Judson, ed. *The Arts and Crafts Movement in*
    America 1876-1916. Princeton, NJ.: Princeton University
    Press, 1972.

Commons, John R. *Races and Immigrants in America*. New York:
    Augustus M. Kelley Publishers, 1967.

Conrat, Richard and Maise. *Executive Order 9066: The Internment*
    of 110,000 Japanese-Americans. San Francisco: California
    Historical Society, 1972.

Counts, Charles. "Written for Rose." *Craft Horizon*, June 1966:
    36.

Eaton, Allen H. Beauty *Behind Barbed Wire*. New York: Harper & Brothers, 1952.

_____. *Beauty for the Sighted and the Blind*. New York: St. Martin's Press, 1959.

_____. *Christmas Letters*, 1931-1962.

_____. *Handicrafts of New England*. New York: Harper & Row, 1949.

_____. *Handicrafts of the Southern Highlands*. New York: Russell Sage Foundation, 1937.

_____. *Handicrafts of the Southern Highlands*. New York: Dover Press, 1973.

_____. "Immigrant Arts in America." *School Arts* 32 (1933): 323-25.

_____ . *Letters to Eric Allen*, 1 June 1920 - 5 June 1924.

_____. *Letters to Clementine Douglas*, 1934-1962.

_____. *Letter to Marian G. Heard*, 3 February 1951.

_____. *Letters to Eleanor Roosevelt*, 1937-1940.

_____. *Memos to Shelby Harrison*, 1929-1944.

_____ . *The New England Exhibition and the American Handicrafts Movement*. Worchester Art Museum Catalog, 1943.

_____. *The Oregon System: The Story of Direct Legislation in Oregon*. Chicago: A.C. McClury & Co., 1912.

_____. *An Outline of the Origin and Development of the Department of Art and Social Work in the Russell Sage Foundation* as formally discussed with the Trustees, 18 May 1944.

_____ . *Promotion Flyer*, 1951.

_____ . *Proposal* to Russell Sage Foundation, 1944.

_____. *Resignation letter to Board of Regents of The University of Oregon*. Eugene, Oregon, 4 October 1917.

Eaton, Allen H. and Crile, Lucinda. *Rural Handicrafts in the United States*. Washington, D.C. :United States Department of Agriculture in Cooperation with Russell Sage Foundation, 1937.

Eaton, Allen H., and Harrison, Shelby. *Welfare Problems in New York*. New York: Welfare Council of New York, 1926.

Eaton, Elizabeth. *Letter to author*, 21 June 1976.

Eugene Morning Register. *Anniversary Edition*, 1904.

Eugene Register Guard. *13 November 1949*, 28 February 1952.

Gaston, Joseph. *The Centennial History of Oregon*. Chicago: S.J. Clark, 1912.

Glenn, John M.; Brandt, Lilian; and Andrews, Emerson. *Russell Sage Foundation 1907-1946: a History in Two Volumes* New York: Russell Sage Foundation, 1947.

Grodzins, Morton. *Americans Betrayed*. Chicago: University of Chicago Press, 1949.

Grubbs, Frank L., Jr. *The Struggle for Labor Loyalty: The A.F. of L. and the Pacifists, 1917-1920*. Durham, NC: Duke University Press, 1968.

Hansen, Marcus Lee. *The Atlantic Migration 1607-1860*. New York: Harper Torchbooks, 1940.

Heard, Marian G. *Taped interview*, July 1975.

Hess, J. William. *Letter to author*, 7 July 1975.

Japan Society, Inc. *Membership letter*, 20 August 1951.

_____. *Report of the Arts and Literature Committee*, 12 November 1952.

Jones, George W. *Letter to author*, 19 May 1975.

Kenyon, Walter J. *The First Years in Handicraft*. New York: Baker and Taylor Company, 1899.

Krenk, Marvin and Mary. *Interview*, June 1980.

Leighton, Alexander H. *The Governing of Men*. Princeton, NJ: Princeton University Press, 1945.

Levine, Marguerite L. *Letter to the author*, 21 July 1975; with attached memo from K. F. Gruber, 24 January 1963.

Lomax, Alfred L. "Union Woolen Mill Company: A Successful Decade." *Oregon Historical Society* 53 (1952): 90-102.

Macomber, Ben. *The Jewel City*. San Francisco and Tacoma: John Williams, Publisher, 1915.

Manzanar *Free Press*, 1 January 1944.

Mattil, O. J. *Taped interview*, July 1975.

Minnesota University. *Immigration and American History*. Minneapolis: University of Minnesota Press, 1961.

Morgan, Lucy. *Gifts from the Hills*. New York: The Bobbs-Merrill Company, Inc., 1958.

Museums and the Handicapped. Smithsonian Institution. Washington, D.C.: U.S. Government Printing Office, 1977.

Okubo, Mine. *Citizen 13660*. New York: Columbia University Press, 1946.

_____. *Letter to author*, 2 June 1975.

Old Oregon, December 1949.

Oregon Journal, 4 September 1917.

Oregon State Legislature, *Journal of the House*, 1907-1917.

Oregon *Voter*, 11 May and 3 November 1917.

Pennington, Clement Johns. *The Beginnings and Development of Crafts in the Curriculum of the Public Schools of the United States from 1900-1930*. DEd dissertation, Pennsylvania State University, 1975.

Pitman, Louise. *Taped interview*, July 1975.

Rainey, Mr. and Mrs. David. *Interview*, June 1980.

Roosevelt, Eleanor. *Letter to Allen Eaton*, 7 September 1937.

Russell, George William. *National Being*. Dublin, Ireland: Munsel, 1917.

Sage, Margaret Olivia. *Endowment letter*, 19 April 1907.

Schaefer-Simmern, Henry W. "Art Education as a Social Problem." Appendix to *Allen Eaton Memo/Proposal*, 16 May 1939.

_____. *The Unfolding of Artistic Activity*. San Francisco: University of California Press, 1948.

Schedig, Walter. *Weimar Crafts of the Bauhaus*. New York: Reinhold Publishing Corp., 1967.

Schmitt, Martin. *Letter to author*, 4 June 1975.

Sinclair, Upton. *The Goose-Step: a Study of American Education*. Rev. ed. Girard, KS: Haldeman-Julius Publication, 1923.

Spectator, The, exact date unknown.

Stevens, Bernice. *Interview*, July 1975.

_____. *A Weaving Woman*. Gatlinburg, Tennessee: Buckhorn Press, 1971.

Takashima, Shizuya. *A Child in Prison Camp*. Montreal, Canada: Tundra Books, 1971.

Todd, Frank Morton. *The Story of the Exposition*. New York: G.P. Putnam's Sons, 1921.

University of Oregon. Eugene, Oregon. *Board of Regents Misc. Records*, Vol. 5, p. 373, 376.

Villard, Oswald Garrison. "The Allen Eaton Case." *The Nation*, November 15, 1917.

"Voyage to India." *Craft Horizons*, May/June 1960, p.54.

Webb, Aileen O. "Allen Eaton, 1878-1962." *Craft Horizons*, January 1963.

Books By Allen H. Eaton
(Arranged in Order of Publication)

The Oregon System: The Story of Direct Legislation in Oregon. Chicago: A.C. McClury & Co., 1912.

Welfare Problems in New York City. New York: Welfare Council of New York, 1926.

A Bibliography of Social Surveys. New York: Russell Sage Foundation, 1930. (with Shelby M. Harrison)

Immigrant Gifts to American Life. New York: Russell Sage Foundation, 1932.

Handicrafts of the Southern Highlands. New York: Russell Sage Foundation, 1937. Dover Press Edition, 1973.

Handicrafts of New England. New York: Harper & Brothers, 1949.

Beauty Behind Barbed Wire: The Arts of the Japanese in Our War Relocation Camps. New York: Harper & Brothers, 1952.

Beauty for the Sighted and the Blind. New York: St. Martin's Press, 1959.

t h e   a u t h o r

David B. Van Dommelen is professor emeritus at the Pennsylvania State University. He and his wife Michal live in the mountains of Central Pennsylvania where he runs a private design firm. Photo by Donna Ralston-Smolko.

Other books by David B. Van Dommelen

Design at Work: Its Forms and Functions, (with E. Adams and G. Pappas), Center for Continuing Liberal Education, The Pennsylvania State University, 1961.

Decorative Wall Hangings: Art With Fabric, Funk & Wagnalls, New York, 1962.

Walls: Enrichment and Ornamentation, Funk & Wagnalls, New York, 1965.

Designing and Decorating Interiors, John Wiley & Sons, Inc., New York, 1965.

New Uses for Old Cannonballs, Funk & Wagnalls, New York, 1966.

Doughboy Letters, VDI Press, State College, Pa., 1978.

North to the Past, VDI Press, State College, Pa., 1997.

i n d e x

Page numbers shown in *italic* indicate images.

c o l o p h o n

Allen Eaton's favorite typeface, Caledonia (the Latin name for Scotland), was designed by William A. Dwiggins for Linotype in 1939. This book is set using the New Caledonia typeface from Adobe, Inc. Adobe's description notes that: "In the late 1980s, Linotype released New Caledonia, removing some of the constraints placed on the original design when it was first produced in metal."

ORDER ADDITIONAL COPIES OF

ALLEN H. EATON

Dean of American Crafts
by DAVID B. VAN DOMMELEN
(ISBN 0-9711835-9-7)

from THE LOCAL HISTORY COMPANY
Publishers of History and Heritage
www.TheLocalHistoryCompany.com
Sales@TheLocalHistoryCompany.com

ORDER FORM—PLEASE PRINT CLEARLY

NAME _____

COMPANY (if applicable) _____

ADDRESS _____

CITY _____ STATE _____ ZIP _____

PHONE _____ PLEASE include your phone number so we can contact you in case there is a problem with your order.

Please allow 2-4 weeks for delivery. Prices are subject to change without notice. All book sales are final. US shipments only (contact us for information on international orders). Payable by check, money order, or Visa/MC/Discover in US funds (no cash orders accepted).

PLEASE SEND _____ copies at $29.95 each .... Subtotal: $_____

Sales Tax: PA residents (outside Allegheny County) add 6% per copy
Allegheny County, PA residents add 7% per copy $_____

Add $5 shipping/packaging for the first copy and $1 each additional copy $_____

TOTAL AMOUNT DUE: $_____

PAYMENT BY CHECK/MONEY ORDER:
____ Enclosed is my check/money order for the total amount due made payable to: *The Local History Company.*

PAYMENT BY VISA OR MASTERCARD Credit Card:

Bill my _____ Visa _____ MasterCard   Account # _____
(Address above must be the same as on file with your credit card company)

Expires _____ Name as it appears on your card _____

Signature _____

Mail or Fax your order to: The Local History Company
(FAX 412-362-8192)   112 NORTH Woodland Road
                             Pittsburgh, PA 15232-2849
         Or—Call 412-362-2294 with your order.